MW01505874

PurimBursts II

Sarah Yehudit Schneider

✳ *Published with the holy help of* ✳

The dear and beloved Lurie Family

Friends of

A STILL SMALL VOICE

Correspondence Teachings in Classic Jewish Wisdom
Jerusalem

Published by:

A Still Small Voice
Chabad 90/16
Jerusalem 97500
ISRAEL

TEL/FAX: (02) 628-2988
EMAIL: smlvoice@netvision.net.il
WEBSITE: www.astillsmallvoice.org

הרב לוי יצחק הלוי הורוויץ בס"ד

דער באסטאנער רבי

Grand Rabbi Levi Y. Horowitz

"I feel that this endeavor is very worthwhile. Even the person with greater background will find new thoughts to contemplate and study in this work through the author's focus on how to use the practices of Torah, prayer, and mitzvot to enhance one's relationship with Hashem."

Rabbi Levi Y. Horowitz (The Bostoner Rebbe)

Aish HaTorah
College of Jewish Studies

"I hold Ms. Schneider in very high esteem and can verify that she is highly respected, reliable, and that she approaches her work with an exceptional intellectual motivation which constantly inspires...it is rare to find someone with such depth of knowledge and commitment to bringing back the pride of our heritage."

Rabbi Noah Weinberg, Dean

NEVE·YERUSHALAYIM

"...she enables the serious student to taste the vibrant spirituality of Judaism that permeates even its most basic principles of faith and practice through her creative treatment of the subject, and emphasis on internalizing the information... I warmly recommend A Still Small Voice to anyone who is interested in enriching their lives with the spiritual content of Judaism."

Rabbi David Refson, Rosh Yeshiva

THE HERITAGE
בית המסורה
HOUSE

RABBI MEIR SCHUSTER
FOUNDER & DIRECTOR

RABB. AVRAHAM EDELSTEIN
EXECUTIVE DIRECTOR

"Of all our staff in the women's hostel over the years, Susie has stood out as the person most capable of answering the wide range of questions that have come up. She has worked hard both to acquire the necessary knowledge and to find ways of translating this into the language of the unaffiliated."

Rabbi Meir Schuster

כפר חב"ד, טל' — 351 03-9607
מגדל־עדר, גוש עציון. ד. נ. צפון יהודה
טל' — 204 02-932

"I have been impressed by Susan Schneider's knowledge of Torah in general and Chassidut in particular, as well as her command of the English language and ability to deftly convey even very abstract ideas clearly... I trust her ability to develop and elaborate raw ideas into cogent, well-researched expositions."

Rabbi Yitzchak Ginsburgh

Network of ☺ CONSCIOUS JUDAISM

"This course draws on mysticism and mainstream Judaism, and covers a wide range of essential issues and practices. It is not pushy, but it demands time, and thought and commitment... You will be challenged and stimulated... It is very provoking for the beginner and advanced alike."

Rabbi David Zeller

ACKNOWLEDGEMENTS

Hashem should bless every single one of His people—and in particular the holy souls who helped to bring these Torah teachings into the world—with "light, blessing, mirth, pleasure, glory, good assembly, song, delight, goodness, dew and rain, salvation, sustenance, learning, contentment, consolation, joy, exultation, redemption, cheerfulness, upright pride, ingathering of exiles, acceptance of prayer, favor, satiety and peace." (From the Yom K'Purim Mussaf prayer).

יהי רצון מלפניך [שתהא לנו ולכל] עמך בית ישראל בכל מקום שהם... **אור, ברכה, גילה,** דיצה, **הוד,** ועד טוב, זמרה, חדווה, **טלולה** וגשומה לברכה, ישועה, **כלכלה, למוד,** מנוחה, נחמה, ששון, עצלון, פדות, צהלה, **קוממיות, קבוץ** גליות, **קבול** תפילות, רצון, שובע, **שלום,** ותוליכנו קוממיות לארצנו...

To the generous Lurie family for enabling this publication.

To Leah Shoshana Weil for her hours of editing work.

To Uriella Sagiv for her astute editing advice.

To Avital Levi for masterfully (and gracefully) taking care of business.

To Ruth Shlossman for her blood, sweat and *cheers*.

To Sarah Weil, Talya Lev and David Abutbul for creating a beautiful website to spread the word.

To Yael Yunger for managing the website.

To my teachers and students throughout the world for encouraging the work and bringing it to life by applying it into the nitty gritty of their lives.

כל הנשמה תהלל י-ה הללוי-ה

TABLE OF CONTENTS

I PurimBasics

The Purim Story…………………………………………1

Laws and Rituals of Purim Observance………... 7

Purim Themes…………………………………... 9

II PurimBursts

PurimBurst, 2001
HOW TO IDENTIFY THE CROWN PRINCESS………..15

PurimBurst, 2002
MESIRUT NEFESH AND THE ORAL TORAH………… 21

PurimBurst, 2003
TORAH OF SOULS……………………………..……..29

PurimBurst, 2004
I AM THE FIRST AND I AM THE LAST……………   37

Purim Mantra in Haiku, 2005
THE *CHASHMAL* CHARIOT …………………………..46

PurimBurst, 2005
    A TIME FOR SILENCE, A TIME FOR SPEECH 47

PurimBurst, 2006
    ANGER DRIVES THE PLOT........................... 57

PurimBurst, 2007
    THE BOOK OF ESTHER AS A MAP OF FEMININE
    DEVELOPMENT 71

Purim Mantra in Haiku, 2008
    ALL FOR ONE & ONE FOR ALL...................... 99

PurimBurst, 2008
    IF YOUR ENEMY IS HUNGRY GIVE HIM BREAD..... 100

PurimBurst, 2009
    THE POWER OF A GOOD EYE...................... 120

PurimBurst, 2010
    UNTIL YOU DON'T KNOW..........................132

III Glossary and Backmatter

    Glossary 144

    A STILL SMALL VOICE Program Resources....... 162

    About the Author............................... 168

The Purim Story[1]

Jeremiah's foreboding predictions proved true. The first Temple was ravaged. Yet he also prophesied its rebuilding at the end of seventy years. The Purim story opens with Achashverosh, king of the Persian Empire, celebrating the failure of Jeremiah's second prediction to materialize. Seventy years had passed and there was no sign of the Temple's reconstruction. The Jews, exiled from their land, lacked the resources to initiate the project themselves.

Achashverosh held an extravagant six-month feast to celebrate his rise to kingship[2] and

---

[1] This is the Purim story that appears in the Bible as the Book of Esther. The Oral Tradition includes many teachings on these events that do not appear in the biblical text. The Purim story, as presented here, incorporates many of these midrashic elaborations.

[2] Rashi, on Esther 1:3.

successful claim to the Temple's holy objects.[3] In the midst of his drunken reverie the urge arose to show off his queen and Achashverosh ordered her to appear naked before his guests.[4] Queen Vashti refused and was executed for her insubordination.

The king then launched an empire wide search for a new queen. Scouts dispersed throughout the land to round up all the beautiful women. Each had one chance to excite the king's fancy. If her evening passed without a marriage proposal from the king, the girl was sent to the king's harem where she lived the rest of her life cloistered and forgotten.

Among the contenders was Esther, a Jewish orphan, raised by her uncle Mordechai. When Esther was snatched by the beauty scouts, Mordechai adjured her to conceal her Jewish roots. The king was smitten by her grace and ended his four-year search by crowning Esther queen.[5]

A man named Haman became chief advisor to the king. Drunk with newfound power Haman ordered all citizens to bow when he passed.

---

[3] Midrash Esther 1; TB Megilla 12a.

[4] TB Megilla 12b; Midrash Esther 3.

[5] The banquet occurs in the 3rd year of Achashverosh's rule, Esther is crowned in the 7th year and Haman issues the decree for Jewish destruction in the 12th year.

Mordechai, the chief rabbi of the exiled Jewish community and (unbeknownst to Haman) the uncle of Queen Esther, refused to oblige. He considered it a semblance of idolatry and forbidden for him as a Jew.

Haman raged at the insult and sought revenge not just against Mordechai but against his entire people. Haman cast lots (literally, *purim*) to determine the best date to enact his evil scheme. He bribed Achashverosh to issue a royal decree: Eleven months from now, on the 13th of Adar, citizens throughout the Persian Empire are urged to exterminate all the Jews in their midst.

When the edict went out the Jews donned sackcloth and cried to their God. Mordechai instructed Esther to approach the king to confess her Jewish roots and beg for mercy.

Esther balked, preferring to wait for the king to invite her on his own initiative. All royal attendants, including the queen, were barred from entering the king's chambers unbidden. To do so meant certain death *unless* the king extended his scepter and allowed the intruder to live.

Nevertheless, Mordechai insisted that Esther take the risk and go *now*. Esther instructed the Jews to fast for three days while she prepared her soul for the challenge. The fate of her entire people rested on her ability to maintain a constant state of grace with the King above and the king below.

Esther donned royal attire and entered the king's chambers. Achashverosh, moved by her holy beauty, extended his scepter and asked to hear her request: Up to 50% of the kingdom and it would be granted. Instead she invited the king and Haman to a second wine party later that afternoon.

At their luncheon the king again urged Esther to voice her request. Again, she solicited the king and Haman to a wine party the following day.

Haman, exploding with self-importance from the queen's exclusive invitations, could hardly contain his conceit. Travelling home he encountered Mordechai who still refused to bow, Haman snapped into a narcissistic rage and wanted revenge *now*. Haman prepared a large gallows and planned to secure the king's permission to hang Mordechai the very next day.

That night the king had insomnia and asked his attendants to recite pages from the palace diary. They read a report (from several months back or perhaps even years) where Mordechai saved the king's life by exposing an assassination plot. The king inquired whether Mordechai had been rewarded for his loyalty. The answer was no.

Just at that moment Haman appeared in the king's courtyard seeking permission to hang Mordechai. Before Haman could voice his request the king commanded him to dress Mordechai in royal attire and lead him on a decorated horse through the city streets announcing, "This is how the king honors his favored ones."

Haman, humiliated, had no time to process this turn of events as the couriers rushed him to lunch with the royal couple. The king again requested that Esther voice her wish. Dramatically she answered, "I plead for my life and the life of my people. We have been condemned to death by an evil man...the man sitting right here among us, the wicked Haman."

The king rose in a rage against Haman's trickery and stomped to the garden. Haman approached Esther to beg for his life but he tripped and landed on her couch. Just then the king re-entered and saw Haman lying upon his queen. Haman was hanged on the very same gallows that he had prepared for Mordechai.

Achashverosh explained to Esther that a decree of the king, once issued, cannot be revoked. Achashverosh could not simply cancel the edict calling for Jewish extermination. Instead they sent a new pronouncement permitting the Jews to arm themselves and slay any persons attempting to harm them on the 13th of Adar, the date originally set by Haman's lots (*purim*) for Jewish extermination.

When Adar arrived most citizens understood that it was not the king's wish to slaughter the Jews and so they refrained from aggression. All who still chose to attack were repelled and annihilated. In the walled capital of Shushan the battle for Jewish survival lasted a second day.

The Jews created the holiday of Purim to celebrate their miraculous rescue from extermination on the 14th of Adar (and in walled cities like Shushan on the 15th for the threat there lasted another full day).[6]

---

[6] Purim is one of the Seven Rabbinic *Mitzvot*, which means its observance does not derive from Hashem's Sinaic word, but was instituted later by the Sanhedrin (High Court of Sages) and carries a Rabbinic-level status instead of a Torah-level one.

Laws and Rituals of Purim Observance

1. One must hear the Purim story read aloud twice from a *kosher* scroll: once in the evening and once during the day.[7]

2. On the day of Purim one must send two portions of different, ready-to-eat foods (preferably via a third party intermediary) to at least one friend or neighbor.[8]

3. One must distribute charitable gifts to at least two poor persons on the day of Purim. It is preferable to spend more money on gifts to the poor than on feasting and food gifts.[9]

---

[7] *Shulchan Arukh* (SA) 687, 689:1.

[8] Ibid., 695:4; *Mishneh Brura* (MB) 18.

[9] Ibid., 694:1,2; MB 1,3.

4. One must eat a celebratory meal during the day that includes bread.[10]

5. One drinks wine at this celebratory meal "until he can no longer distinguish between blessing Mordechai and cursing Haman."[11] According to some it is sufficient to drink just a bit more than usual and fall asleep. The important thing is that one's intentions be spiritual, that it be a "rejoicing of the *mitzvah*" and that one be careful regarding prayer, blessings and other *mitzvot*.[12] Anyone who, under the influence of drink, does not properly praise God is forbidden to drink more than usual.[13]

---

[10] SA 695.

[11] MB 695:2; MB there.

[12] SA 695:2 and Rema there; MB 4, 5 and *Biur Halacha* there.

[13] *Sheiltot* and *HaAri*.

Purim Themes

1. **Purim – definition.**[14]

   Purim is a Persian word that literally means *lots* and refers to Haman's casting of lots to determine the best date to launch his plot to exterminate Jews.

2. **Upside down.**

   In the Purim story everything turns upside down. Haman's evil intentions backfire and cause his own demise. The gallows that he built to hang Mordechai are, in the end, used for him and his sons. His detested enemy, Moredechai, supplants him as second to the king. Those who attempted to exterminate the Jews were themselves annihilated. The Jews' terror and sackcloth turned to joy and celebration.

---

[14] Esther 9:26.

3. Amalek, the national identity of Haman, the antagonist of the Purim story.

Israel was born as a people when they crossed the Red Sea. Amalek was the first nation to assault them after their miraculous passage. The wonders that accompanied Israel's exodus from Egypt proved God's love for them, yet Amalek was undeterred. Without a trace of compunction its soldiers attacked straight away. Amalek's distinction as "first" to assault Israel (God's chosen ones) attests to their rotten core. Amalek thus embodies the deepest and most irredeemable root of evil[15] in the universe. All of evil's secondary manifestations will be cleaned and salvaged. Only Amalek has no portion in the world to come—only its citizens are categorically rejected as converts

---

[15] Evil is here defined as the illusion of separation and independence from God. The word 'illusion" is significant since nothing can actually be separate from God for God is one. To the extent that something presents the appearance of self-containment, self-sovereignty, and multiplicity it partakes of the quality of evil. Conversely, to the extent that it communicates through itself the truth of God's goodness, oneness, compassion and generosity it partakes of the quality of holiness.

to Israel.[16] In the Torah's lexicon of symbols Amalek becomes the token of pure evil. Haman, the archenemy of the Purim story, was an Amalekite. Today there is no living nation carrying that name.

4. The upside down relationship between Purim and Yom Kippur.

Yom Kippur with its fasts, repentances and intensive prayer is the holiest day of the Jewish year. Purim is the exact opposite. Its lighthearted celebrations, with everyone silly and tipsy, is downright irreverent by Yom Kippur's standards. Yet here again the truth is upside down. R. Isaac Luria notes a similarity in the Hebrew words for Purim (פורים), and Yom Kippur (יום כפורים)—the difference between them simply being the letter כי (which, as a prefix, means, "like" or

---

[16] The prohibition against marrying people from the nations of Ammon and Moav only applies to the males, and not the females as seen in the story of Ruth. In fact, both males and females from these two nations can convert but the males can only marry other converts while females can marry full status Jews. Amalekites, however, are not accepted as converts at all. *Mechilta: Mesechet Amalek* 2 (toward end) as brought by R. Tsadok HaKohen, *Yisrael Kedoshim*: p. 131 (original edition), and repeatedly throughout R. Tsadok's writings.

"similar to"). This hints to the secret relationship between these two days where, Yom Kippur becomes, literally, the day that is כ׳ (like) Purim. This statement attributes the primary (and trend-setting) holiness to *Purim.* Yom Kippur (as it were) strives for Purim's sanctity but never quite measures up. It comes close enough to be called "like Purim" but not more. There are many wonderful explanations of why this is so.

5. **"Until you don't know…"**

The Code of Jewish Law includes the following *mitzvah* in its listing of Purim practices: "One is obligated to drink wine on Purim until you don't know the difference between blessing Mordechai and cursing Haman." This phrase, "until you don't know…" carries a wealth of mystical associations explicated in chassidic and kabbalistic writings.

✴ The highest root of the soul, the point where it is hewn from the pure simple oneness of God, is called רישא דלא אתידע (The Unknowable Head). It is the source of pure and simple faith; knowing beyond mind, experiencing beyond awareness the truth of God, and the truth of God's oneness, goodness, and love. On Purim the lights of this highest root of soul, the Unknowable Head, fill the world. We express this below by entering the state of consciousness defined by the Code of Law as "*until you don't know* the difference between curse…or blessing…"

✴ This state of "not knowing" that is accessed on Purim through inebriation is also accessed by the throwing of lots (*purim*). Some questions are beyond the rational mind's capacity to fathom all of their relevant factors. One solution is to throw lots, asking for God to make His will known through their outcome. The person throwing lots admits that he "doesn't know" which option is the right one. *Ayin* (אין) means literally, nothing. When a person cast lots he stands in a place of "not knowing," aware that he is "nothing" before God. By the principle of resonance his "nothing" invokes the Divine "Nothing," the Unknowable Head, the innermost pure core of Divine Presence.

6. Haman homonyms.

There are three homonyms of the Hebrew word, המן (*haman*): (1) It spells the proper name of Haman, the archenemy of the Jewish people in the Purim story. (2) These same three letters also appear in the Genesis story when HaShem rebukes Adam and Eve after they eat from the Tree of Knowledge. Here, the Hebrew letter, ה, at the beginning of the word, המן, indicates that the sentence that follows be read as a question. The next two letters, מן, mean "from." Consequently, in this verse, המן means, "From...?"[17] (3) The manna that sustained the Israelites throughout their forty-year desert sojourn is called מן (*maan*). The Hebrew letter, ה, at the beginning of a word often serves as a definite article turning the noun that follows from general to particular; for example "*the* table" instead of "*a* table." Consequently המן means "*the* manna (*maan*)."

---

[17] Genesis 3:11. "And [God] said, 'Who told you that you were naked? Have you eaten from the tree from which I commanded you not to eat?'"

PurimBurst, 2001 / 5761

Inspired by R. Tsadok HaKohen

(רסיסי לילה לב, נב)

And the king loved Esther more than all the other women and she won his grace and favor more than any of the other maidens, so that he set the royal crown (מלכות כתר) upon her head and made her queen…(Esther 2:17).

As the world nears its end of days the nation of Israel (like Esther) prepares to inherit its own crown, its culminating glory, its messianic kingdom. And then, with quiet grace, it will assume its mystic role as queen to the holy King of Kings.

As below so above—as with a person, so with a people. A child is born with a halo of soul-lights that can't fit inside due to its state of immaturity.

As the child grows, matures and wisens these soul lights gradually integrate into its personality. Eventually, in the course of its life, nearly all the lights that had previously surrounded the infant now fit inside and shine through the eyes of the venerable elder. The last lights to enter are those called *crown*. In the *sefirotic* scheme *crown* is the innermost root of the soul. When the *crown* (כתר) comes in, the *kingdom* (מלכות) of heaven finally dwells below (כתר מלכות). An embodied *crown* marks an enlightened soul.

Exactly so in the macrocosm. The entire Jewish people comprise a single entity called *Knesset Yisrael*, the Greater Community of Israel. Each individual is but a cell in this larger collective *Adam*. *Knesset Yisrael* was born when it crossed the Red Sea and over the next 3,317 years it has grown, matured and hopefully wisened. Now as we approach the end of days our own crown of lights is soon to enter. This will bring an entirely new

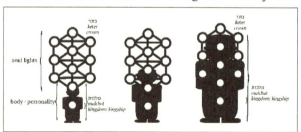

capacity of consciousness called the Messianic Era. It will be distinguished by a deeply integrated knowing that God is one and good and all there is, with Israel as His bride.

R. Tsadok explains that whenever a new awareness enters the nation of Israel it stimulates a projection of contrary assertions among the other nations. Their denials cast doubt on the original truth. Is it a heavenly revelation or a delusion of grandeur?

Amalek (the archenemy of Israel) has the same numerical equivalent as ספק (doubt) for that is precisely his expertise. Inside each nation is a spark of Amalek that masterminds its psychic battle with Israel, its media blitz of lies and half-truths that cripple the brain's ability to recognize truth. Thus, says R. Tsadok, the mind cannot defeat Amalek, only the heart with its mysterious capacity for *knowing* truths that cannot be proved. This is especially so in the final battle over the *crown*. Israel asserts that God chose them as proprietors of His Holy Land, Holy City and Holy Mount. While any God-serving citizen may dwell there the people of Israel are its divinely designated heirs. The nations assert that God chose *them* as proprietors of these same holy environs, that *they* are the legal guardians. On the surface both claims have equal merit. It's one word against the other. Yet in truth one is the crown princess and the other a pretender to the throne.

How does the real heiress prove her identity when an imposter has stolen her story? Not by words, for whatever she says the usurper claims the same. Not with guns, for everyone knows that might does not make right. Not with a vote, for the issue is truth, not popular opinion.

The strategy is simple, says R. Tsadok, for lies are a surface phenomenon. They only prosper in regions far from the core of Infinite Light. Amalek keeps the crowd enthralled, their eyes glued to the surface where appearances rule and there's no way to tell a mask from a face.

The difference between truth and lie can only be seen by looking in, away from the surface, to the heart (Shmot 3:3,4). And it takes a heart to know a heart. And even more, to know when there is no heart. Truth has a root that draws its light from the central core of Infinite Light and that is its heart. Lies, says the Talmud, are "towers floating in air." They are not plugged into the core. They have phantom roots which means they have no heart.

And so, says R. Tsadok, Amalek crumbles before a knowing heart. Truth yearns to be seen and even scrutinized, for that is what sets it free. A lie when fathomed disintegrates for as soon as awareness hits layers deeper than its false root it ceases.

As long as the battlefront stays on the surface, with words and claims and counterclaims; as long as the task is to prove to others the truth of her

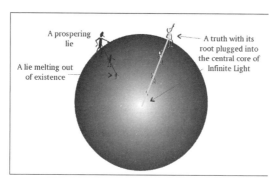

appeal the princess cannot win. But as soon as she shifts her focus inward, tracing her truth to its root and planting her feet firmly there, the princess cannot lose. Amalek has no defense against a knowing heart. He cannot fight where he does not exist.

Knowing is an active force in the universe. It alters the landscape of energies and events in exact proportion to its depth of integration. Yet, knowing is only thus potent if it is absolutely impervious to external censure. It must be completely self-referenced, looking only to God and Torah for its validation.

On Purim the lights of knowing beyond knowing (עד דלא ידע...) shine from the crown and stream through the world. Let them fill your mind and heart and even the spaces between the molecules of your being with the deeply integrated knowing that you are a cell in the collective community of Israel, a divinely appointed guardian of the holy land, a crown princess to the King of Kings, a spark of the Shekhinah herself. Dance, kiss the ground, shout, thank the Lord; there is no greater blessing than this. May the strength and joy born from this knowing "find grace in the King's eyes. May He set the royal crown (כתר מלכות) upon [our] head and make [us] queen."

PurimBurst, 2002 / 5762

Inspired by R. Tsadok HaKohen[18] and R.R.M. Luria[19]

Letters were sent...to all the king's provinces...to destroy, slay and exterminate all Jews on the 13th of Adar [11 months from then]...Mordechai immediately bid Esther to approach the king, to plead for her people...[Esther proposed an alternative strategy, preferring to wait for the king to invite her at his own initiative.] "All royal attendants are barred from entering the king's chambers unbidden," she replied. "To do so means certain death unless the king extends his scepter and allows the intruder to live. It is now already thirty days since I was last summoned by the king."...Mordechai replied, "If you persist in keeping silent at this time relief and deliverance will come to the Jews from some other place while you and your father's house will perish."[20]

---

[18] *Pri Tsadik*, Adar [ו];

[19] *Ora v'Simcha*, (p. 97-99)

[20] Esther 3:12 – 4:14

W hy did Mordechai insist that Esther go *now*, unbidden? Esther agreed to approach the king but wanted to wait until called by him, which would surely be soon. Why imperil her life needlessly? *Halacha* forbids one from taking unnecessary mortal risks. Since the genocidal decree would not take effect for nearly a year, it did not seem to justify a life-threatening exploit. Mordechai's gamble only makes sense to those who know the secret, that Purim is one with the Oral Torah.[21]

HaShem revealed two Torot at Sinai: the written text and its oral explanations, which include all the levels of implication intended by each word. [22] The lights of every teaching that would (and could) ever unfold from these first Five Books all descended in that blazing moment of revelation.[23] In *chassidic* writings Oral Torah is a code word for each person's unique perspective on truth that is *their* "letter of the Torah."

---

[21] Shabbat 88a; *Pri Tsadik*, Adar 6.

[22] TB, *Brochot* 5a.

[23] *Sifra* 105a; TB *Megillah* 9b; TY *Peah* 2:4; *Torat Kohanim* (end of *Bekukhotai*); *Midrash Tehillim* (*Mizmor* 12).

The Written Torah was a gift of guidance on a silver platter; the Oral Torah "is only truly acquired by one who dies for it." [24] Yet, as we know, there are two kinds of death: physical death and ego death and the latter is more bitter than the former. In ego death one lives with discomfort day in and day out. Unlike physical death it does not bring release, rather the opposite. In ego death one stews in the juices of pain, frustration or humiliation until a solution is found. This might simply be a shift in attitude, behavior, or circumstance. At worst relief might only arrive with the moment of death.

The Written Torah specifies three very limited circumstances where one must be willing to "die for it" and the death here mentioned is a physical one. [25] In all other instances life takes precedence and one is *required* to transgress the Torah's law to save one's skin. [26] In contrast the Oral Torah requires a *constant* willingness to endure ego death as the non-negotiable precondition to acquiring its sweet, soul-satisfying truths. One must be willing

---

[24] TB *Brochot* 43b, *Torah Temima* on *Bmidbar* 19:14, *Tanchuma* on *Bereshit*.

[25] Rambam, Mishna Torah, *Sefer HaMada* 5:2.

[26] Ibid, 5:1

to bear physical privation, indignities and forego all manner of ego-gratification when truth and integrity require that path.[27]

At Sinai we accepted our Written Law with open arms: "Whatever you ask from us, HaShem, we will gladly do and trust that it will eventually make sense."[28] But the Oral Torah was a whole different matter. Who could accept its ultimatum of unrelenting self-sacrifice? That would be suicidal. Yet HaShem did not take no for an answer. Instead He coerced us with blinding revelations that reduced all negative options to nonsense.[29] We agreed, but a contract entered under duress is not legally binding.[30]

Mordechai understood that the time had come for Israel to accept the Oral Torah with whole and willing hearts. Yet why should now be different? Its price tag had not changed. Esther was the key. Mordechai saw that she could bring down the lights that would open the hearts of her people to the wondrous blessing of their Oral Torah. If just once they could taste its nectar they'd be hooked.

---

[27] TB *Brochot* 5a.

[28] Exodus 24:8.

[29] TB Shabbat 88a; Maharal, *Or Chadash*.

[30] TB Shabbat 88a.

There is no purer joy than discovering truth. And since, as the Talmud declares, "There is no truth except Torah,"[31] whenever a person learns a lesson or grows from their suffering they generate a piece of the Oral Torah.

Kabbala refers to the Oral Torah's lights as *resurrecting dew*[32] for two reasons:

1. Unlike rain, which obviously descends from above, dew seems to appear out of nowhere, from below. Similarly, the Written Torah obviously came from HaShem in a moment of heavenly revelation. Not so the Oral Torah, defined as the cumulative body of creative insights pressed from the hearts of Jews striving to live with integrity according to the truths they absorbed at Sinai.[33] These epiphanies also seem to arise on their own,

---

[31] TY *Rosh Hashanah* 3:8.

[32] Tikunei Zohar 19; TB Shabbat 88b, *Pri Tsadik*, Adar [ו].

[33] The Oral Torah includes two primary categories. The first is the authoritative chain of oral tradition that started with Moses and passes from mouth to ear, master to disciple, from Sinai until today (*Sifra* 105a). The second is the accumulated wisdom of individual Jews from that point onward no matter what their standing in the community or level of religious observance (*Pri Tsadik*, *Chanukha*, [2], p. 143; Adar [1]; and many other places.).

from below, from the people themselves. It is not obvious that they too are divinely bestowed.

2. Nature abhors a vacuum. As soon as an empty space appears it exerts a suction that draws into itself exactly those lights that match *its* particular shape. This is the secret of potent supplication. A master of prayer knows how to craft these dark holes of longing into powerfully articulated entreaties—carefully sculpted vessels—that pull down the lights that are exactly configured to fill their empty space of lack. This same principle applies to the blessed revelations that comprise the Oral Torah. Its dew drops of supernal sweetness originate in the highest realms of Divine reverie. There is only one vessel with enough vacuum-power to tug these lights down into this world. That vessel is ego-death (and also physical death when it sanctifies God's name). This dew, when it descends, revives the soul. The person returns to life resurrected, renewed, enlightened and transformed.

Morechai insisted that Esther go, *now,* precisely because of the peril entailed. When Esther entered the king's chamber unbidden she risked physical death and faced certain ego death for, at that moment, she lost the possibility of ever resuming her marriage to Mordechai, of ever again knowing his embrace.[34] Her fate was sealed. She must live out her days as Achashverosh's wife.

Mordechai chose Esther for the task because he saw that she was not just a person, she was a *meta*-soul. Through her the Jewish people were held together as a higher order unity called the *Mystical Body of Israel.* Their souls were so entwined with hers that the resurrecting dew she pulled down as the fruit of her self-sacrifice opened every heart to the Oral Torah. Mordechai's plan worked. The Jews accepted their Oral Torah, קימו וקיבלו[35], in joyful celebration with free and willing hearts.

Let it be your will, HaShem, that on this holy Purim—when inebriation also counts as ego death— that we draw down Your most prized stash of resurrecting dew called the Torah of Mashiach, with its paradigm-shifting secrets about how to purge evil without also destroying healthy flesh. This much we've learned: We can't nuke it, we can't sit at a table and negotiate with it and we can't ignore it. There is a solution but its lights are not in the universe yet. They

---

[34] TB *Megilla* 13a.
[35] Esther 9:27.

are waiting for an empty-space-of-longing that has enough vacuum-power to pull them through. All the resources of the Jewish people (material, emotional, mental and spiritual) are focused on this question and dedicated to its task. May the vessel created by our combined efforts and accumulated ego deaths—by the broken hearts of our mourners, the broken lives of our wounded, the daily sacrifice of all who bear the yoke of Torah, the sleepless nights of our leaders who carry the burden of life and death on their shoulders—may all this finally pull down the dew of relief, salvation and Mashiach NOW.

PurimBurst, 2003 / 5563

Then the King conferred with His sages (**חכמים**), experts in reading the times, for such was the King's practice, to consult with the masters of law and judgment...Memuchan declared before the King...let it be written...and never revoked...that Vashti never again appear before King Ahashverosh and let the King transfer her queenship to another who is better than she. (Esther 1:13-19).

Everyone knows that whenever the word, *King*, appears in the Book of Esther it is a double-entendre that applies both to Ahashverosh and to the heavenly King, the King of Kings, the Blessed Holy *One*.[36]

And so says the Zohar:[37] HaShem does not pass judgment upon wrongdoers without first

---

[36] ספר הפליאה - ד"ה טצי"ץ ט תשעה, צ תשעים, ץ ט. ;מדרש אבא גוריון פרשה א

[37] Zohar (*Midrash Ne'elam*) I:104b.

consulting His *tsadikim*. Their role is to expound the virtues of the accused and plead for acquittal. The Zohar is clear: A *tsadik* is either defending or silent. One who accuses is rotten somewhere and guilty of corruption. After all, says the Zohar, if someone had called down justice upon Terach for his idolatry (which carries the death penalty), Avraham would not have appeared, the twelve tribes would never have been, the Torah would not have descended, King David would never have lived and Mashiach would never be born.

These sages (חכמים) with whom the King consults are called the *eyes of the people*.[38] This is because HaShem views the nation through their peepholes. This is a holy burden and a deadly serious one. According to the Baal Shem Tov, if HaShem brings harsh decrees upon the Jewish nation it is because the sages have lapsed in their duty and impugned guilt upon the people, even if only a sector of them.

We are told that, "*this* opposite *this* HaShem created the world."[39] Everything holy has a dark counterpart somewhere in the universe. And so, in the Purim story every character has its alter-ego

---

[38] SHS Rabba 1:64; 4:2; 5:16; Ari, Etz Chayim 8:11; etc.

[39] Kohellet 7:14.

from the other side. Mordechai has Haman, Esther has Vashti, and even HaShem has Ahashverosh. And now we see that the sages have a shadow side as well, represented by the King's inner council that passed a harsh judgment on Vashti, the accused. They showed the king their allegiance by imposing death for even a minor affront to his pride. For one who serves the shadow king that *is* the way to curry favor. Yet the opposite is true for ministers of the heavenly King's court.[40] HaShem loves His people far more than his glory (i.e. His Torah),[41] and seeks any pretext to be lenient. In his own words:

> The way of mankind is to ascribe a higher status to love of Torah than love of each other …I [HaShem] say that love of My people is the priority[42].

The task of *His* legal team is to devise ways to reframe the offense that minimizes guilt or even

---

[40] *Pesikta Rabotai*, 41:4.

[41] The equation of HaShem's "glory" to Torah, comes from: פרדס לרמ״ק שער כ״ז ערכי הכנויים, ראה כבו״ד ותור״ה.

[42] Tanna deBe Eliyahu Rabba, 14

gives it a positive spin.[43] R. Levi Yitzchok of Berditchiv was a master of this stratagy.

What distinguishes a true sage (חכם) from a shadow imposter? Heichal HaBrocha[44] explains that the former's expertise in defending the people comes from reading the Torah of souls as well as the Torah of ink on parchment. Just as there are 600,000 letters of the Torah, so are there 600,000 root souls in the spiritual community of Israel. Each individual Jew that comes into the world embodies some unique piece of one of these sixty myriad letters. And so, says R. Tsadok,[45] just as there is a scroll of ink on parchment, so is there a scroll of souls that includes the entire unfolding of generations. The sum total of the soul-sparks of Israel comprise a single and complete Torah...the *real* Torah...the one that HaShem studies on His side of the *mechitza*.[46] Yet this scroll of souls is virtually impossible to read. Its lights are too bright and too complex for the human mind to fathom, at least at its earlier stages of development. And so,

---

[43] ר' יצחק אייזק יודה יהיאל סאפרין, נתיב מצוותך ו,י ו מגילת אסתר, א:יג.

[44] ר' יצחק אייזק יודה יהיאל סאפרין, היכל הברכה, מגילת אסתר, א:א.

[45] ר' צדק הכהן, צדקת הצדיק אות קצ"ו (סוף).

[46] ר, שלמה עליאשאוו, ספר הכללים, כלל ח"י ענף י' סימן ג' אות י"ב.

the Torah of ink on parchment serves as its commentary, presenting the same teachings in a more condensed and readable format. In our immaturity we don't see that the commentary is only an aid to enable our access to the real Torah, the Torah of souls. But as we grow and mature and move toward perfection we come to see things more from HaShem's perspective which assigns priority to the people whose souls are actually the inner lights of the Torah now manifest to us as ink on parchment. From HaShem's perspective love of the people Israel *is* actually love of Torah. The whole point is to learn to read the *living* Torah that shines through each person as he or she dances out the teaching of the letter that is the root of his or her soul.

And so, Heichal HaBrocha adds a beautiful twist to his interpretation of the verse:[47]

גל עיני ואביטה נפלאות מתורתך :

Open my eyes and I will behold the wonders of your Torah.[48]

He splits the word for wonders (נפלאות) in half so that it reads as two words, נפל אות, which means

---

literally "fallen letter." The translation of the verse now becomes:

> Open my eyes, that I will behold the fallen letters of your Torah [that are concealed within every moment, thing and person around me].

There is no question that every letter of the Written Torah is a treasure. And just as we break our teeth and lose sleep and even risk our lives, generation after generation, to drink from its living waters so must we cherish the scroll of souls, for each one of *its* letters is also a wellspring of blessed light.

And there is no question that every sentence of our Written Torah is bursting with holy teachings. Even the verses spoken by evil men like Lavan and Billam and Essav.[49] Even Pharaoh's audacity: "Who is HaShem that I should heed His voice...I do not know HaShem and I will not let Israel go." Even that irreverence is holy writ no less than the *Shema* or Ten Commandments.

But what does that mean for a Jew whose soul is rooted in that outrageous verse (or another of its kind)? What can those words possibly look like

---

[49] ר, שלמה עליאשאוו, חלק הבאורים, שער העקודים א:ז.

embodied as a Jewish life? What contradictions must such a person bear? It's a strange role, yet someone has to play it. No letter can be missing from either Torah scroll. The Talmud declares: wherever there is Torah, there is truth."[50] This means that even the most wayward, self-hating Jew has some insight that they are teaching the world. The work of a *talmid chakham* of the Torah of souls is to find that truth and bless it.

HaShem says in no uncertain terms: עמך כולם צדיקים[52]. Every one of the nation of Israel is a *tsadik* in training. And since nothing is ever all or nothing it must be that some part of us is already there. That means that our voice also gets counted when HaShem consults His *tsadikim* before passing a decree upon His people. We are His "experts in law and judgment." He adds up all of our "advices" (which are the judgments we constantly make about each other) and formulates a verdict for the nation as a whole. In this way HaShem sees the world through our eyes, yet how many people a day do each one of us sentence to Siberia or worse? This is no way to bring redemption. We pray for Mashiach and yet "counsel" against it when we find no redeeming value in the very

---

[50] TY Rosh Hashana 3:8.

people that must merit the redemption for which we yearn. As ministers to the heavenly King we must learn to love each letter of the Scroll of Souls as much as we love each letter of our Written Torah.

Memuchan was a master of harsh judgment, a sage of the shadow side. Mordechai was a master of compassionate judgment, a sage of the Torah of souls. As the Book of Esther declares: "Mordechai sought the good of his people and spoke words that brought peace [to each and every one of them] as if they were his own seed."[51]

Let it be that when the consciousness-altering lights of Purim stream through the world, that for that day and those hours, we rise to the occasion and judge every single Jew for good, praying and laboring to find the truth that is the teaching of their particular letter in the scroll of souls. The resounding consensus of that positive judgment from the King's advisory council should compel the heavenly court to rule that it's finally time for Mashiach NOW.

גל עיני ואביטה נפל-אות מתורתך

---

[51] Esther 10:3.

PurimBurst, 2004 / 5564

And [Mordechai] brought up Hadassah, that is, Esther, his uncle's daughter; for she had neither father nor mother. (Esther 2:7)

וַיְהִי [מרדכי] אֹמֵן אֶת הֲדַסָּה הִיא אֶסְתֵּר בַּת דֹּדוֹ כִּי אֵין לָהּ אָב וָאֵם.

Esther's tale is the story of all women and since the Jewish people are compared to the moon (which is feminine) it is also their saga as well.

The Book of Esther is a historical narrative that occurred between the years 367 - 357 BCE.[52] Yet there are moments in time that are nearly transparent. The veil lifts and behold, real people with real lives are suddenly part of a holy drama

---

[52] 3394 – 3404 since the birth of Adam (the first human being) in the Jewish counting of years.

that conveys the most sublime and eternal truths through the mundane facts of their unsuspecting lives. Esther's tale is a masterpiece in this regard. Stick a pin through any page and secrets spill out on the other side.

There are two words in Hebrew that contain the same three letters, rearranged. They are אין (*ayin*) and אני (*ani*). The first means *nothing* and the second means *I* and *ego*. The first is a name for the most transcendent and unknowable level of Divine Being. The second refers to the illusion of oneself as an independent entity separate from God. In general a spiritual path moves from *ani* to *ayin*, from self-absorption to self-surrender. The kabbalists associate *ayin* with the crown of the head and *ani* with the soles of the feet (and even the ground beneath them). You can't get farther apart than that. Yet they are really just opposite poles of Divine expression for one thing is certain, "There is

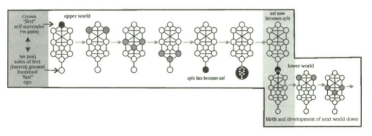

nothing but God."[53] And so HaShem Himself affirms: "I am first and I am last [I am the crown and I am the footstool], besides me there is no God."[54]

I used the masculine pronoun here out of habit, because it is our convention to refer to God as He. Yet in fact this verse is spoken by the feminine face of God, the holy *Shekhina,* the cosmic She (at least according to R. Shlomo Elyashuv, the master kabbalist known as the Leshem).[55] He explains that the unfolding of worlds happens in stages. Each downward step produces a denser reality. Slowly spirit congeals into matter as it passes through the spiritual, mental, emotional and physical planes. Each level births the one below it. Thus the footstool (*ani*) of the upper world becomes the crown (*ayin*) of the next world down. And yet, says the Leshem, the inner core of that newly formed crown disappears and descends through a hidden passageway, only to reappear heavily disguised as the barren ground that is the lowest point of that very same world. Whereas the crown is a radiant source of bounty, barren ground is bereft of even its

---

[53] Deut. 4:35.

[54] Isaiah 44:6.

[55] R. Shlomo Elyashuv, *The Diminishment of the Moon*, chapter 10.

basic needs: seed and moisture. No one would know that these two are really one. Its truth is deeper than the eyes can see.

This constant motion between crown and footstool, *ayin* and *ani,* ruler and servant, is the feminine's kabbalistic role (according to the Leshem).[56] It contrasts with the masculine power which, as the central pillar, is stable and solid, like a backbone that holds the body upright. He is birthed by the crown and stands upon the footstool. His strength is his unswerving commitment to truth.

The feminine's experience is the opposite, for she is in constant motion. She is the first and she is the last, and then the first again. She is both the highest (אַיִן) and the lowest (אַנִי). The former is her secret truth, the latter is what meets the eye. She appears as a footstool, and that is her service. Yet her essential self, says the Leshem, is actually higher than all whom she serves, for she is their source on high. Everything traces its roots back to her. Whatever exists no matter how lofty, she preceded it, and even more she birthed it into the world. This split between inner truth and outer role, inner royalty and outer dependence is a paradox that agitates at the core of every woman's soul. The

---

[56] Ibid.

hidden fact of woman's royal ancestry could be the most well kept secret in the universe. Before there was even the thought of creation she inhabited the pure realms of infinite oneness called אין (*ayin*).

And this brings us to Esther for she embodies the Divine feminine in this holy drama. Hechal HaBrocha proves this by reading the verse above in a way that is perfectly consistent with the Hebrew, but expresses an entirely new idea.[57]

כִּי אֵין לָהּ אָב וָאֵם.

Because Ayin *is* her mother and father.

This verse (says he) is teaching that Esther was birthed from pure, Divine oneness. She is a direct descendent of the One Who Transcends All.[58] "She has no mother and father" because she *is* the אין ב״ה[59] expressing itself as אני. And so true to her archetype, she was also a captive woman in the king's court.[60] To be sure she was the queen but this

---

[57] R. Yitzchak Yechiel Safron, *Ketem Ofir*, 2:7.

[58] The Ari does not present any gilgulim for Esther, which is very unusual.

[59] אין ב״ה means the NoThing, Blessed be He. The phrase, ב״ה (Blessed be He) indicates that we are referring to a Divine and superconscious Being and not just an inanimate void.

[60] In verse 2:7, Esther is actually called יפת תואר (beautiful of appearance), which is the same term the Torah uses to indicate the captive woman in Deut. 21:11.

was against her will. Esther loved another and was forced to marry Achashverosh. Crown — footstool, *ayin — ani.*

Now why did Mordechai insist that Esther be the one to risk her life to save the Jews? Everyone knows that HaShem controls the hearts of earthly kings. Why couldn't Mordechai use prayer or kabbalistic meditation to approach the heavenly throne himself and appeal to the King of Kings for mercy? Certainly a *tsadik* of his stature knows the way to *PaRDeS* and could have prevailed.[61]

It seems that HaShem wanted both kings to be appeased (both He and Achashverosh)...for real. It seems that Israel's coming of age demanded that they align the physical with the spiritual and the political with the holy in a way that *truly* satisfied the interests of both. What an impossible mission. And it seems that Esther's familiarity with *ani* and *ayin* and her ease of negotiating between them made her uniquely suited for the undertaking.

When Haman maligned the Jews to Achashverosh he said:

---

[61] PaRDeS is a term that hints to the kabbalistic meditation where a person's soul travels up through the various chambers of the *heavenly palace*.

"There is a certain people...whose codes are different from everyone else; and they do not keep the king's laws; therefore, it does not profit the king to tolerate them." His argument prevailed and "The King [indicating both Achashverosh and the King of Kings] removed his signet ring ... and said, 'Do with them as you see fit.'"[62]

The Jews now faced annihilation from both worlds. They incurred the earthly king's wrath because they held fast to their Torah and refused to assimilate. They incurred the heavenly king's wrath because they were lax in their practice and had begun to assimilate, even if only at their edges.

Both kings had to be appeased but each demanded precisely what the other forbid. What an impossible knot. And this was Esther's mission: To find the truth (and the words to express it) that would ring in the heart of both kings, each with their polar opposite interests, and all this without compromising her integrity one iota. Interestingly, the sentence she speaks contains both the words *ayin* and *ani.*

כִּי נִמְכַּרְנוּ **אֲנִי** וְעַמִּי לְהַשְׁמִיד לַהֲרוֹג וּלְאַבֵּד וְאִלּוּ לַעֲבָדִים וְלִשְׁפָחוֹת נִמְכַּרְנוּ הֶחֱרַשְׁתִּי כִּי **אֵין** הַצָּר שׁוֶֹה בְּנֵזֶק הַמֶּלֶךְ

---

[62] Esther 3:8-11.

For we are sold, I and my people, to be destroyed, slain and annihilated. But if we had only been sold as slaves and maid servants I would have kept my silence. Instead the enemy has **not** sufficiently recompensed the king for the damage [that will be incurred to him by the Jews' annihilation.][63]

With *ani* Esther appeals to the earthly king. Achashverosh does not care about the Jewish people but he does not want to lose Esther, his chosen one.

With *ayin* she appeals to the heavenly king and her last phrase could be retranslated applying Haichal HaBrocha's technique:

כִּי אֵין הַצָּר שֹׁוֶה בְּנֵזֶק הַמֶּלֶךְ

The ayin [the contrite and whole-hearted submission of Israel's will to *HaShem* expressed through their fasting and teshuva] even though it was prompted by distress [and not by their own initiative] nevertheless, does still compensate for the "debt" they incurred to the heavenly King [through their earlier, wayward behavior].

Esther's formula succeeded. Both kings were appeased. Esther found a strategy that convinced both the heavenly and earthly powers (even though the latter was as corrupt and drenched in self interest as Achashverosh).

---

[63] Esther 7:4.

History repeats itself. Again, Israel is pressed between the contradictory demands of its heavenly King and an unholy fellowship of world rulers. What a set-up. Yet if Esther is our prototype then HaShem is asking us to pursue a similar strategy. Like master locksmiths we are challenged to find the combination of truths that will release the deadlock, satisfy both Kings and bring redemption NOW. And again if Esther is our prototype the solution will be a feminine approach born in the heart of one who knows the mystery of *ani* and *ayin* from the inside, from experience. And just as "Mordechai did exactly as Esther commanded him,"[64] we must give voice to our feminine wisdom and be willing to follow its lead.

This Purim, when everything turns upside down, when ani becomes ayin, and ayin becomes ani, and HaShem lets loose His treasure chest of hidden lights into the world, and we all stretch to receive them, let it be that at least one among us catches the spark that solves the current paradox that is the key to our redemption, and that the rest of us holy and unholy kings should see its truth and accept its guidance.

---

[64] Esther 4:17.

A Purim Mantra in Haiku, 2005

The *Chashmal* Chariot

When you stand before God, be
Like a woman who
wills and yields at the same time.

PurimBurst, 2005 / 5565

When Mordechai conveyed to Esther... "If you remain silent at this time relief and deliverance shall come to the Jews from another place and you and your father's house will perish"... Esther responded... "Very well. I will go to the king, contrary to the law, and if I die I die..." Esther donned royalty, and stood in the inner court of the king's palace, opposite the king's chamber... (Esther 4:13-5:1).

When Esther learned of the king's decree to annihilate the Jews of his kingdom she intended to plead for her people as soon as he summoned her to his presence. His invite was sure to come soon and meanwhile she would wait and pray. Why imperil her life for nought? *Halacha* prohibits unnecessary mortal risks. Since the genocidal decree would not take effect for close to a year, it did not justify a life-threatening exploit.

Yet Mordechai insisted that Esther go *now*, unbidden. This was not a time for silence he urged, *this* was a time for speech.

Modechai did not follow the precedent of Egypt.[65] In that grand exodus, the Jews got trapped between the sea and Pharoah's horde and the people cried to heaven for release. There, HaShem actually rebuked Moshe for resorting to prayer (מה תצעק אלי) and thus Moshe hushed the people to silence (אתם תחרישון).

The Zohar[66] explains that the Israelites' escape from Egypt was a delicate surgery, a complicated extraction that required a precise balance of *chesed* and *gevurah* (generosity and stringency). These attributes formed HaShem's double-edged scalpel which cut through the tangles and allowed their release. Our self-absorbed prayers disturbed the fragile balance by invoking excess judgment. They dulled the scalpel and nearly spoiled the *tikun*. The clumsier the surgery, the more loose ends remain to be worked out through exhausting ordeals that can drag on for millennia.

---

[65] Exodus 14:10-15.

[66] Zohar II: 47a-48b.

The Zohar[67] also brings a second reason for this call to silence. The Providence coming down in that dramatic moment at the Red Sea was from the most inner core of Divine influence, called *Atika*. Its lights transcend reward and punishment and lie beyond the range of prayer. The only way to access them, maybe, is through silence. This we learn from another instance where Moshe asks why the righteous suffer, a query whose answer also pulls from the level of *Atika*, and here too HaShem commands silence: שתוק כך עלה במחשבה לפני.[68] Rebbe Nachman of Breslov reads this not as a rebuff but as an invite.[69] HaShem was teaching Moshe a practice that could bring him to the inner chamber where the answers to his question lie: "Silence. That is the way up to the inner point of Divine thought (called *Atika*)."

Similarly then, when HaShem demanded silence at the sea He was instructing the Israelites in this same spiritual practice; the service of silence (חש) which is different from the service of prayer.[70] As King Solomon wisely observes, עת

---

[67] Ibid; Sira D'Tsniuta 178b.

[68] TB *Menachot* 29b. "Silence! Thus it arose in thought before Me." In other words, "Shut up! This is what I decided…period."

[69] *Likutei Moharon* 64:3

[70] R. Tsadok HaKohen, *Dover Tsedek*, p. 131.

לחשות עת לדבר. ("There is a time for silence and there is a time for speech.")[71] The Red Sea was a time for silence. Israel's Purim crisis was a time for speech. How did Mordechai know?

Hechal HaBrocha reads the secrets and spins the following tale.[72] Esther was a prophetess of the highest rank. She was an expert in the kabbalistic practice of *yichudim*, a secret mystical technique that can draw the super-conscious lights of pure grace (*Atika*) down into the lower worlds. These are the same lights that parted the sea. They are beyond nature and easily override it. Relying on precedent, Esther formulated a plan: She would harness the mystical chariot and go up into the silence. Using imagination to transcend imagination she would pull down a miracle of the sea-parting type. Esther was a master of this technique. She was certain to succeed.

Yet Mordechai saw that times had changed; HaShem was calling for something new. With one thousand years of soul-purifying *mitzvot* under their belt, the Jews were poised to make a quantum shift. The time had arrived to accept, with whole and willing hearts, their Oral Torah, the living and

---

[71] Ecc. 3:7.

[72] R.Y.Y.Y. Safron of Kamarna, *Ketem Ofir* (on Esther) especially 4:11-5:4.

evolving body of teachings that expand and elaborate the written text.[73] This was at least as momentous as Sinai. God's word was set to descend another notch and fuse deeper still with the Jewish soul. If Israel passed this test prophecy would give way to *intuitive insight* (חכמה). HaShem's revelations would condense like dew on the hearts of His people seeding insights from the inside out. The Oral Torah, says R. Tsadok, is the accumulated body of wisdom pressed from the hearts of Jews striving to live with integrity to the truths they absorbed at Sinai.[74]

Always, at moments of quantum shift, someone must rise to the tip of *this* world, reach up through the heavens and pull the lights down.

---

[73] R. Tsadok HaKohen, *Pri Tsadkik*, on Purim where he explains the comment of TB Meg. 16b on Esther 8:16, "To the Jews there was light (אורה)...' Rav Yehuda says, *Light* refers to Torah..." Yet since light is written in its feminine form, אורה instead of אור, it refers to the feminine Torah, the Oral Torah.

[74] The Oral Torah includes two primary categories. The first is the authoritative chain of tradition that started with Moshe and passes from master to disciple until today (Sifra 105a). The second is the accumulated wisdom of individual Jews, no matter what their standing in the community or level of religious observance (*Pri Tsadik*, Chanukha, [2], p. 143; Adar [1]; *Likutei Maamarim* p. 80-82; *Yisrael Kedoshim* p. 152. and many other places).

Esther was called to perform this feat. At Sinai there was a pyramid of ascent. The people stood below in their designated places at the mountain's base. The seventy elders climbed a little higher. Aharon and Yehoshua higher still. Yet Moshe, alone, went up through the clouds to the peak, to the King. And so now, the time had arrived to pull the Oral Torah down into the hearts of the people and Esther was the chosen one. Alone and uninvited, she must risk her life to approach the king for unlike its holy written counterpart "the Oral Torah is only acquired by one who dies for it."[75]

Esther's mission required that she embody exactly what she hoped to bring down. That's what contact means in the world of lights and souls. Only things that are similar can touch. Esther had to listen *and* to speak at the same time for that is the secret (and definition) of the Oral Torah. She had to listen to the whisper of truth in her heart and express it through action and speech. HaShem would be her guide, but like manna[76], every

---

[75] TB *Brochot* 43b, *Torah Temima* on *Bmidbar* 19:14, *Tanchuma* on *Bereshit*.

[76] Just as the wandering desert Jews had to trust each day that new manna would come, so Esther had to trust, with each step, that new guidance would come.

moment contained a message of its own. At each step she scanned the horizon for options, waiting for her heart to answer yes and there she would move. An extended fast?...A wine-party for three?...Another? There were no neon signs or prophetic voices (or even a battle plan). Alone with her instincts she had to find God's holy word that speaks through *them* as surely as He spoke at Sinai.

The Megilla reports that Esther appeared before the king "donned in royalty (מלכות)." Hechal HaBrocha explains this to mean that she was wrapped in a shimmering mantle of light, called *chashmal* (חשמל), similar to the bodies of Adam and Chava before their sin. The word *chashmal* (חשמל) is built from two sub-words that have contradictory meanings. *Chash* (חש) means silence and *mal* (מל) means speech. The movement between these two poles is what generates Oral Torah. Listening and speaking; receiving and teaching; surrendering and asserting; accepting and beseeching; איו ואני. Back and forth between the poles at lightening speed until, like a spinning propeller, one enters a vibrant stillness that radiates light.

In modern Hebrew *chashmal* (חשמל) means electricity. In science, electricity refers to a whole spectrum of expression including both visible and invisible light. A science primer explains how to generate *chashmal* (חשמל): "A vibrating magnetic field creates an electric field which in turn vibrates and creates a new magnetic field whose vibrations create still another electric field, ad infinitum. This interplay between alternating magnetic and electric fields is what creates electromagnetic waves (including light)."[77]

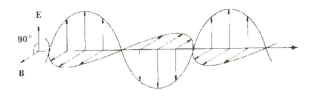

According to Maxwell's theory, light consists of electric fields (E) and magnetic fields (B) that oscillate in unison. Here the electric fields vibrate vertically while the magnetic fields vibrate horizontally.

Esther mastered the dance of *chash-mal* (חש-מל) and wrapped herself in its radiant cloak of grace. She had three days to learn the steps. There was no other way to meet the conflicting demands of her mission:

---

[77] Kaku and Trainer, *Beyond Einstein* (Bantum Books, 1987) p. 24-25.

-Her silence (חש) pulled the redemptive lights of *Atika* down into the world and toppled the genocidal decree.

-Her speech (מל) pulled the Oral Torah (the *speaking* Torah) down into the hearts of the people, which opened the gates to a new age.

-The dance between them (חשמל) was (and is) a path of refining desire (i.e., prayer), deepening silence and opening the mind to *chidushei Torah* (creative revelations of truth).

All this was accomplished without disrupting nature for that is a key feature of the paradigm shift she ushered in where *wisdom* (חכמה) supplants prophesy. As the Talmud declares: "Why is Esther compared to the dawn? For just as the dawn is the end of the night, so is Esther's story the end of revealed miracles."[78]

Apparently HaShem prefers a more "natural" medium of revelation (the insights that arise daily in the hearts of His people) and a more organic path of redemption (one that works in conjunction with nature instead of overriding it).

A person who saves another's life is considered to have birthed them. Rav Tsadok applies this principle to

---

[78] Yoma 29a. Interestingly, the "new day" is the era that is beyond miracle.

Esther.[79] In saving the Jewish people she became the proud mother of us all. Every *mitzvah* performed thereafter gets credited, in part, to her "account". Yet the benefits of this maternal bond go both ways. A child inherits the soul strengths of its spiritual parents. From Avraham we inherit generosity, from Yitzhak dignity from Yakov compassion. And from Esther we inherit a capacity to bear paradox, to dance with it, and to turn it into light, Torah and potent prayer.

Let it be that when the holy lights of Purim stream through the world and HaShem makes an open house in the chamber of Atika, that we seize the moment and rededicate ourselves, with whole and joyous hearts, to our precious Oral Torah that turns each life into a holy site of Divine revelation. May we, who are Esther's spiritual heirs, learn to dance in her footsteps, speak from the silence, and spin the cloak of shimmering light that is our holy birthright.

---

[79] *Tikanat HaShavin*, p. 110 (Bet Yesharim ed.), (but also 107-110).

PurimBurst, 2006 / 5566

Queen Vashti refused to come at the king's command...and the king was *very angry, and his anger burned* in him...And Memucan answered..."Vashti, the queen, has not only insulted the king, but...all the men of the kingdom...For their women will do likewise and it will create an upsurge of *contempt and wrath*."...In those days, while Mordechai sat in the king's gate, two of the king's eunuchs, Bigthan and Teresh, guards of the threshold, were *angry* and sought to lay hand on the king, Achashverosh....And when Haman saw that Mordechai neither bowed nor showed obeisance, he was *full of wrath* [and sought to exterminate not only Mordechai but his entire people]...And the king arose from the banquet of wine *in his wrath* and...so had Haman hanged on the very same gallows that he had prepared for Mordechai. Only then was the king's *wrath* pacified.[80]

---

[80] A compendium of all the verses in the Book of Esther that mention anger.

*E*very moment is a story and every story has a motor that propels its forward motion. In the Book of Esther rage drives each stage of the plot. Achashverosh boils at Vashti's insubordination, orders her execution and initiates a search for her replacement. Haman rages at Mordechai's defiance and secures a decree to massacre both him and his entire people. Bigsan and Teresh seethe with malice toward the king and plot revenge, a plan which Mordechai intercepts and which, unexpectedly, years later, becomes the seed that sprouts redemption. Achashverosh fumes at Haman's inadvertent threat to his queen, and as a result Haman gets hung and the Jews slay all of their would-be attackers. In every instance, a person seeks to relieve his ego discomfort by murdering the immediate cause of his shame or frustration. This is the inner (and universal) mechanism of anger.

The history of kings and nation-states is a chronicle of narcissistic tantrums. Anger's explosive fallout has shaped geo-politics even more than greed. And a disproportionate amount of this wrath gets aimed at Jews. It must be that part of our purpose is to find the most spiritually productive way to play this role and teach it to the world. The Book of Esther provides some clues.

It is known that rage emits a burst of dark energy into the world, an evil wind which is actually a kind of natural resource that can be harnessed to do work and drive change. The Zohar's name for dark lights is *botzina d'kardenuta,* intensely compressed kernals of light as tough as the wheat berries of Kardinuta, a region known for its extreme anti-Semitism and associated with Amelek, the legendary arch-enemy of the Jewish people and forebear of Haman.[81,82]

Each living thing occupies an ecosystem and learns to exploit the resources of that niche to sustain life. Some organisms are remarkably tenacious and manage to endure the most adverse conditions. The ocean's depths, polar caps and barren deserts are the nooks that some creatures call home. Among the human kingdom, the Jewish people inhabit a corner of the universe that is also

---

[81] Zohar I:15a. See Sulam's translation and commentary there.

[82] Encyclopedia Judaica. "…The anti-Jewish attitudes prevailing in eastern-Byzantine (Armenian) provinces made the Targum identify it with the "daughter of Edom that dwellest in the land of Uz" (Lam. 4:21) … Armenia is also sometimes called Amalek in some sources, and Jews often referred to Armenians as Amalekites.

distinguished by severe conditions. Survival has required them to perfect the capacity to transform the intensely concentrated lights that scatter like shrapnel from anger's discharge. They digest these pellets, extract their nutrients and convert their death-wish into life juice. This is an extraordinary gift and it suits their cosmic mission which is "to enable Divinity's full (and manifest) integration into every layer of reality, down to its *lowest edge*."[83]

But what is this "lowest edge" that appears in the fine print of their mission statement? While it is no coincidence that the Jewish homeland contains the lowest point on earth, that does not seem to be the crux. What can higher and lower possibly mean in regards to God when it is a basic principle of Oneness that *HaShem* is equally present in every point of time and space? Kabbala answers that even so, HaShem is not equally revealed throughout creation. In the stepwise sequence of creating our universe HaShem underwent a gradually intensifying series of concealments. Step by step the Infinite Light withdrew from creation and the extent of its

---

[83] Tanchuma, Naso 16: בשעה שברא הקב"ה את העולם נתאוה שיהא לו דירה בתחתונים כמו שיש בעליון. "When HaShem created the world He longed for a dwelling place below in the lower realms like He had in the upper realms.

absence defines the hierarchy of worlds: the less concealed, the higher the world; the more, the lower. The ultimate concealment (and lowest layer) is idolatry, where HaShem is not just invisible, but His accomplishments are actually ascribed to an *other*. And the lowest idolatry is *self*-worship. It lacks even the humility of acknowledging a higher power.

And that was precisely the serpent's ruse when he lured Adam and Chava with the bait, "Eat and you shall be as gods."[84] In fact the serpent didn't lie. The lights of the Fiftieth Gate *were* inside that fruit, lights that conveyed a direct transmission of the deepest secret of the universe.[85] The Fiftieth Gate is the absolute, unqualified, experiential knowing that "there is nothing but God"... including ourselves. And yet only a perfectly transparent (and infinitely elastic) ego can hold that exhilarating truth. You must be invisible to claim your divinity.[86] Those almighty lights will not tolerate the slightest blemish of motive. On the 50th rung even a hairline crack of

---

[84] Genesis 3:5.

[85] Genesis 3:6: The woman saw....that the tree was desired to make one wise (נחמד להשכיל).

[86] And so Esther passed undetected when she entered the king's innermost chamber uninvited.

self-gain will bring shattering to one who partakes of its delights. This we know from experience. Adam and Chava were not just humanity's founding couple, they actually contained the souls of all the people that would ever live. We all participated in their decision to eat and we all suffered the devastating consequences of their misdeed. We tasted those omnipotent lights and the savor of that intoxicating instant remains with us till this very day. Its trace is the (not so) secret belief that the universe ought revolve around *Me.*

And yet, in the following instant, reality shattered. The highest lights plunged to the lowest depths like a toppled wall whose capstones land farthest from the base. The exalted truths of the Fiftieth Gate now, in their fallen state, define the "lowest edge" of the universe, the dregs of idolatrous self-worship. "God is one, there is no other... and I alone am He." Yet this dark sludge is a kind of fossil fuel whose combustion, expressed as burning rage, is a major driving force in the universe.[87]

---

[87] Like a spring compressed and released, these fallen lights of the Fiftieth Gate are driven to return to their root. This is the torque that HaShem planted in the universe to propel its forward motion. For since they now define the lowest edge,

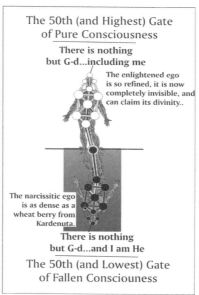

The 50th (and Highest) Gate
of Pure Consciousness

There is nothing
but G-d...including me

The enlightened ego
is so refined, it is now
completely invisible, and
can claim its divinity..

The narcissitic ego
is as dense as a
wheat berry from
Kardenuta.

There is nothing
but G-d...and I am He

The 50th (and Lowest) Gate
of Fallen Consciouness

It is shocking to calculate the quantity of resources (time, space, money, thought, emotions...entire lives) that have been spent reacting to, anticipating, deflecting, preventing, dodging, bearing, avenging, eliminating, reenacting, regretting and healing from rage. Even now in the present, the local enemy calls itself

---

when they return from their exile, which they must do, they will bring everything else up and along with them.

Hamas, a word that in Hebrew means cruel and violent wrath. (It is the only synonym for anger that does not appear in relation to HaShem, which means that it has *no* rectified expression.[88]) The lion's share of Israel's resources—its brain-power, finances, scientific research, psychologists, news reports, prayers, political campaigns and even dinner conversations—revolve around this threat. And so the chain of expulsions, crusades, pogroms, holocausts and jihads remains unbroken until this very day: "In every generation an enemy appears that seeks to destroy [the Jewish nation]."[89] We seem to be a magnet for narcissistic rage. What a strange role and what a massive waste of time ...or is it?

HaShem employs many tools to exert His providential will. Creation is destined to re-attain the Fiftieth Gate and there is no turning back. Yet enlightenment is a labor-intensive process. No one spends that amount of effort without very

---

[88] There is a place for anger but there is no place for חמס.
There are occasions when all the other types of anger:
(קצף, חמה, אף, חרה, כעס, רגז) are appropriate. There is never an appropriate expression of *hamas* (חמס). And so Yaacov actually curses the action of Shimon and Levi because it was motivated by the anger of *hamas* (Gen. 49:5).

[89] *Hagada.*

compelling inducements both positive and negative. HaShem hangs a carrot in front and a flame behind to assure that work gets done. And thank God the Jewish niche is rich in both resources: it has an abundance of delectable carrots and no shortage of motivating flames. But what has shaped us more? Which has produced the greatest positive growth? Is it the carrots or the flames, is it Haman or Mordechai?[90]

Each blast of narcissistic rage spews dark cinders that are paradoxically the highest lights of the Fiftieth Gate fallen, compressed, twisted and disguised as their polar opposite. In Texas they call oil "black gold". So here, Jews have learned to salvage priceless treasures from the sludge of their enemy's self-worship which gets vaporized through the combustion of rage and aimed at their annihilation. Each heirloom is a 50-carat nugget of densely compacted golden light which springs open to reveal its hidden bounty upon contact with the fertile soil of the Jewish soul. There it provides the upward thrust that drives a person to rise to the occasion of their life, despite its ordeals...to turn from the past, inventory the present and start

---

[90] Rav Tsadok comments on Kohellet 1:18 (רב כעס רב חכמה), that the primary motivation for generating wisdom is to deflect an assault of anger.

building. Sometimes the abuse causes such damage that it takes generations to turn and to heal. Perhaps the most precious gift we possess as a people is the spiritual enzyme that digests this dark crud and absorbs its holy drops of energy into our heart, bones, cells and spaces. "And the more they afflicted [the Hebrews] the more they increased…"[91] And because of *this* we continue to rise.

And so on Purim our joy is not that we survived the wrath which boomeranged back and destroyed our enemies instead. That was good news, filled with comic irony, but it is not enough to sustain the high of Purim for generations. Rather the ecstatic and uncontainable joy of Purim is from the paradigm shift that we made as a people, when we extracted the lights of the Oral Torah from that ordeal. This living and evolving body of teachings is an amalgam of heavenly revelations and human realizations. The Oral Torah is not just the authoritative chain of rabbinic commentary. Rather, says R. Tsadok, every person makes a contribution to the Oral Torah. It is the sum total of creative insights pressed from the hearts of Jews striving to live their lives with

---

[91] Exodus 1:12.

integrity to the truths they absorbed at Sinai. The authoritative and unchanging Written Torah clearly originated above and without. The Oral Torah is the exact opposite. Its truths emerge from below and within. HaShem's words form like dew on the heart, nourishing revelations from the inside out. Purim initiated a new age where the boundary between God and man is porous. This is the ultimate reversal. The hate filled rage of idolatrous self-worship transmutes into a fusion of God and man where they really do start to share a common "I", where the human and the Divine really do begin to merge. A person speaks and God's words leave their mouth, they act and it is God's deed they perform. Now *this* is cause for feasting and jubilation.

The Oral Torah is a resurrection of sparks from the Fiftieth Gate that were released by Haman's tantrum and absorbed by the Jews affected by his decree. Yet these most coveted lights come with strings attached. As explained, they will not tolerate even a trace of impure motive so there's always a purchase price. A person must trade a fist-full of ego for a sliver of light from the Fiftieth Gate.

Practically, how does this show in the Purim tale? First, the word rage does not appear in relation to Jews. They did not meet anger with anger and they did not rampage in indiscriminate revenge. But they were also not passive. They designed a strategy that was tough, effective, cost lives, but protected the intrinsic value of life and property wherever possible. Mordechai and Esther could have designed any solution. The king's signet ring was in their hands. They only permitted the Jews to kill those who actually attacked them, despite the king's obvious change of heart. Haman's decree functioned as a "strange attractor." It drew the hate-mongers out from the pack, those who could not control their bloodlust. Once the fantasy of Jew-slaughtering was let loose, there were those who could not hold themselves back. They alone were slain by the Jews on that fateful pre-Purim day. And there was no taking of booty even though it was permitted. This was not a frenzied riot, but a calculated and targeted mission of self-defense with decisions made to minimize collateral damage to the greatest extent possible. This they learned from Avraham whose prayer on behalf of Sodom was a heartfelt plea to eliminate collateral damage for HaShem's *sake*.

Secondly, they looked heavenward and sought the hidden purpose for this ordeal. Even though they were absolutely innocent by *this*-worldly standards, there is always a higher design which if exposed, softens the pain.[92] For example, we understand that when Yaakov stole "the blessing" of Jewish heritage, Essav cried a shofar blast of a cry (ויצעק צעקה גדולה ומרה עד מאד), for he knew the loss was immeasurably great.[93] And even though Yaakov did the right thing, and it was HaShem's will (which makes it a *mitzvah*), and the survival of the people and the planet required exactly that, still, he (we) must pay full dues for the crookedness of the act (even though it was all for HaShem's sake, and there was no other way). Essav's cry echoes through history and is re-paid (at least in part) by Mordechai's cry at the genocidal decree (ויזעק זעקה גדלה ומרה)[94].

And third, the next day the Jews moved on…to inner healing, *teshuva* and celebration. They got to work unpacking their *spiritual* booty, the lights from the Fiftieth Gate that entered their possession *because* they did not take ego gratification from their victory. They accepted the

---

[92] Malachi 4:20: "But to you who fear my name the sun of righteousness shall arise with healing in its wings…"

[93] "And he [Essav] cried a very great and bitter cry" Gen. 27:34.

[94] "And he [Mordechai] cried a great and bitter cry" (Esther 4:1).

gift and burden of their Oral Torah, which reduces to one central point:

The world's understanding of God's ways comes from their observation of our behavior.

Let it be this Purim, when the world turns upside down, and the lights of the Fiftieth Gate stream through, that we fuse together as a people in our joy, the bumps and dips[95] in line this to that, each quirk with an anti-quirk canceling its imbalance, until…we arrive at our true, invisible self, pass through the yesh-detectors[96] and claim our divinity as bride to the King.

---

[95] "Bumps and dips" meaning those with too much ego and those with too little, those leaning to the left and those leaning to the right, those who are introverts and those who are extroverts, etc.

[96] *Yesh* translates as "there is-ness", as something that has density, opacity and physical presence. Here it refers to ego states, quirks or unrectified personality traits.

PurimBurst, 2007 / 5567

Based on the teachings of R. Isaac Luria as presented in
*Kabbalistic Writings on the Nature of Masculine and
Feminine*.[97]

This opposite *this* HaShem created the world."
(Ecclesiastes 5:14)

Everything holy has a dark counterpart somewhere in the universe. And so, in the Purim story every character has its alter-ego from the other side. Mordechai has Haman, Esther has Vashti. And even HaShem has Achashverosh.[98]

---

[97] Sarah [Yehudit] Schneider, *Kabbalistic Writings on The Nature of Masculine and Feminine (*KW)*, (3rd) edition SSV Publications (available at website below).

[98] TB Megilla 10b, ספר הפליאה - ד"ה טצ"ץ ט תשעה, צ תשעים, ץ ט.
האריז"ל - ספר פרי עץ חיים - שער ר"ח ;מדרש אבא גוריון פרשה א
חנוכה ופורים – פרק י'

The Talmud says that the word *king* only refers to HaShem when it is not followed by the proper name of Achashverosh.

The secret is that if you follow the soul thread of each one back up to its root, the hero and his nemesis always merge. Kabbala refers to this shadow-self as the *backside* of a person, his *achorayim* (אחוריים). Just as a back is the place on our body that we cannot see so is this true for a soul. Its backside includes all the sparks that lie beyond the range of its conscious self, all the disowned layers of personality that appear as not-us. The sum total of these not-yet-integrated pieces of soul is what psychology calls the unconscious and what Kabbala calls the *backside* (אחריים).

Megillat Esther is an historical chronicle and a kabbalistic teaching tale. When read from the latter perspective there are three composite characters: the masculine archetype which combines Haman and Mordechai; the feminine archetype built from Vashti and Esther; and the Divine Presence played by Achashverosh and the King (i.e., HaShem). The story becomes a microcosm of the evolving

---

The Midrash says that whenever the word *king* appears (even followed by Achashverosh) it also refers to HaShem.

relationship between masculine and feminine as taught by Kabbala.[99]

In the world of kabbalistic archetypes *man*[100] is stable, enduring, unchanging. He is compared to a tent peg that doesn't budge no matter how strong the winds blow. *Woman*, by contrast, displays the evolving, perfecting, transforming potential of soul. She associates with the moon that is always in motion, waxing or waning as the case may be. Anything that grows or changes displays feminine attributes. Yet people are not archetypes. The Principle of Interinclusion rules the real world. Every human being contains both male and female aspects in varying proportions. Yet archetypes are useful. They portray the elemental forces both in the world and inside our own psyches. They present the big picture that gets lost in the subjectivity of a single generation (or even an entire lifespan).

---

[99] האריי״זל עץ חיים – שער מעות הירח א׳ Ari, *Aytz Chaim, Hechal Nukva, Shaar Miut HaYareach*, chapter 1; Sarah [Yehudit] Schneider, KW pp. 52-98.

[100] The words *man* and *woman,* when italicized, refer to the archetypal masculine and feminine and not to male and female human beings who are much more complicated than their archetypal counterparts.

The Ari describes three general phases in the evolving relationship between *man* and *woman* (which divide into seven substages). Since *woman* is the one in motion this becomes the universal map of her life cycle, which proceeds as follows:

Phase 1 – Initial equality between masculine and feminine.

Phase 2 – Diminishment of the feminine.

Phase 3– Re-attained equality, that is even more consummately equal than was possible before.

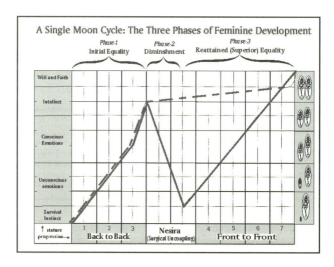

In his model, *woman* first develops a kind of false equality (phase 1), collapses again quite suddenly (phase 2) and starts a new push toward growth and full stature which she eventually attains at the end of her effort (phase 3). These three phases comprise a single moon cycle. They apply on all scales from the inter-included feminine inside every soul, through the span of an individual woman's life, to the history of creation (for the entire period of existence from the beginning of time to its end is but a single circuit of the kabbalistic "moon.").

The source-text for his teaching is the marital saga of Adam and Eve. Tradition teaches that they began as a single androgynous creature whose male and female halves were fused together like Siamese twins along their backsides.[101] God then severed this backwards bond and released them to meet face-to-face as freestanding individuals for

---

[101]"God created *Adam* in His own image, in the image of God He created him; male and female He created them…And the Lord God said, It is not good that the *Adam* should be alone; I will make him a help to match him…And the Lord God made *Adam* fall into a deep sleep…and He took one from his sides, and closed up the flesh. And the side, which the Lord God had taken from *Adam*, He made a woman, and brought her to the *Adam*." (Gen. 2:20-23)

the first time. This is how Jewish tradition interprets the Biblical story of Eve's formation.[102] The kabbalistic term for this surgical uncoupling is *nesira* and it divides the imperfect equality of phase 1 from the consummate equality of phase 3.

––––––––––––––––––––––––––––––

[102] The passage above (footnote 101) contains an inconsistency. Its first verse describes Adam as both male and female.

> God created *Adam* in His own image, in the image of God created He him; male and female He created them.

This treats the word "*Adam*" as a generic term, like "human being," that includes both genders. Translated thus, the verse reads, "God created human beings in His image, with male and female genders He created them."

And yet, shortly thereafter the Bible comments that Adam is alone and seeks a mate, for there are no other human beings around and none of the animals feels like a soul partner:

> And the Lord God said, "It is not good that *Adam* should be alone; I will make him a help to match him…"

This passage clearly suggests a contrary interpretation, that "*Adam*" is a single creature and not a species comprised of two (or more) individual members. Otherwise he would not be alone. But if Adam is a single entity what does the first verse mean when it states, "male and female He created them"?

Reconciling this discrepancy, Tradition teaches that the first human being was an androgynous creature like a Siamese twin, with male and female halves joined at the back. HaShem then caused an anesthetic sleep to descend upon this bi-gendered Adam and surgically severed its halves, creating two separate and free-standing entities called Adam and Eve.

In the graph above the bottom axis maps *woman*'s life path, which proceeds from 1 to 7 and divides into three phases. The vertical axis measures *woman*'s "spiritual height" in relation to *man*, her maturity of consciousness and her relative access to intellectual (and prophetic) resources. At a glance, Phase 1 and Phase 3 are nearly the same. Each marks a gradual course of growth from diminishment toward fullness of stature as illustrated on the far right. In contrast, the bottom row's three divisions measure a more intangible property. They distinguish a front-facing encounter from a back-facing one. Just as the front of a person includes the face with its eyes and sense organs that define its field of awareness, so is this true for an *archetype*. The *front* associates with conscious will, mindful action and rectified behavior; the *back* with all that is unconscious, compulsive and reactive.

In a *back-to-back* relationship the couple's primary bond of attraction derives from projections, obsessions, addictions and narcissistic cravings. In contrast, a *front-to-front* relationship is one where the couple shares common goals and a mutuality of desire. The Hebrew term for face (פנים) stems from the same root as the word for inwardness (פנימיות). A front-facing relationship is one where the couple's insides meet and their souls unite.

The superiority of Phase 3 derives from its preeminence on *both* scales: *woman* and *man* are spiritual equals and they meet face to face, will to will. In Phase 3 *man* and *woman* unite from the crown of their heads to the soles of their feet, from outer skin to inner core. In the Ari's own words, "*Man* and *woman* finally stand face to face and completely equal."[103]

Yet, wedged between Phase 1 and Phase 3 is the most dramatic interval of *woman*'s life, the surgical uncoupling that releases the pair to meet in a face-to-face union.[104] For *woman*, this boon

---

[103] האריז״ל – ibid; Schneider, KW, p. 73.

ותכלית גידול שלה, הוא שיהיה בה כל היי״ס שלה, ותהיה עם זי״א פב״פ שווה לגמרי, וישתמשו ב׳ מלכים בכתר א׳, שהוא מה שקטרגה הירח כנודע.

[104] *Nesira* is actually a gradual process that proceeds throughout the whole course of a relationship. The couple meets as best they can, face to face, but there are layers of each that are hidden even to themselves, let alone to the other. These parts remain back to back until the consciousness of the individuals (and of the couple) permeates there and then they begin their journey of turning which starts with *nesira*. See Ari's model of the 10 stages of *nesira* that occur between Rosh HaShanna and Yom Kippur (*Shaar HaKavvanot, Drush Rosh HaShana* 1).

comes at great sacrifice. Its quantum leap forward on the quality scale entails a major backslide on the vertical scale that measures woman's access to higher lights. Her stature shrinks, even as she gains the possibility of real (and equal) relationship, a prospect that only appears when a couple sees each other's face and loves each other's soul.

Purim marks the *nesira* between Israel and HaShem, asserts Kabbala. [105] At Sinai we received the Written Torah, the holy string of letters and teachings that contains the truth of the universe condensed into its five short books. Its words are fixed and final. An error in even a single letter disqualifies the entire scroll. The Written Torah does not permit tinkering or innovation. Before this holy writ we can only hear and obey; there is nothing to add.

The Oral Torah is a whole different revelation and this is what we achieved on Purim. The Oral Torah is living and evolving. It is the sum total of creative insights pressed from the souls of Jews striving to live their lives with integrity according to the truths of Sinai. HaShem's words form like dew on their hearts, nourishing revelations from the inside out. It is here, in the quiet of this holy

---

האריז"ל - ספר פרי עץ חיים - שער ופורים [105]

dialogue, that we meet our Creator face to face. In the amalgam of heavenly revelations and human realizations we attain a consummate union that is truly give-and-take.

And it came to pass in the days of Achashverosh.[106] The Purim plot follows this three-phased map. It opens with the players in neurotic codependence. In back-to-back attachment individuals do not differentiate for their backsides are enmeshed. No one knows where *he* ends and another begins. Each projects his flaws, fears and shame onto someone else. The system operates more like a herd than a collection of individuals. Haman and Achashverosh are especially fused in this way. They function as a single character: Haman is the will and Achashverosh is the brawn. Haman has his own vendetta against Vashti, for she insulted his pride.[107] The king becomes a mask that Haman wears to enact his revenge. Who killed Vashti? Was it the king or Haman? The Midrash leans toward the latter reading: "Achashverosh put his wife to death on account of his friend."[108]

---

[106] ME 1:1.
[107] MRE 4:6.
[108] MRE 1:1.

Where is the hint to Esther in the Torah? It derives from the verse: *"And I [God] will surely hide My face* (הסתר אסתיר פני)".[109] HaShem is dragged into this motley mix.[110] The term *God* gets encrusted with narcissistic projections when His *face* withdraws and He meets creation back to back (הסתר אסתיר פני). In this fallen state God's glory is reduced to a spitting image of the ego in its most grandiose display. And so in the Purim story HaShem appears in the unflattering role of a foolish, hedonistic and megalomaniacal king.[111] It is no surprise that Haman, the most narcissistic of the bunch, grabs the job of managing the King's PR. HaShem's image gets branded by Haman's string of fiery missives that disseminate through the kingdom.

[Achashverosh] displayed the riches of his glorious kingdom and the splendor of his excellent majesty for many days… And Vashti the queen also made a banquet for the women in the royal palace…[112]

Just as Achashverosh opened six treasuries, so Vashti opened six treasuries. Just as he went

---

[109] TB Chulin 139b.

[110] Song of Songs 7:6.

[111] TB Meg. 10b.

[112] ME 1:4.

to all kinds of expense, so she went to all kinds of expense. Just as he feasted after the style of the Land of Israel, so she feasted after the style of the Land of Israel. Just as he wore the high-priestly garments, so she wore the high-priestly garments.[113]

In a back-to-back relationship each seeks to outshine the other. The couple competes for attention and power. The goal is to amass the lion's share of narcissistic supply.

Achashverosh the king, commanded…Vashti the queen to appear…with the royal crown…But Queen Vashti refused to oblige.[114]

The king actually commanded Vashti to appear naked, clothed *only* in the royal crown…Vashti sent her refusal in the strongest terms, "Go tell your stupid master that his orders are outrageous. I am the daughter of the great king Belshazzar…In the house of my father, your master would not have been good enough even to clean out the stables![115]

---

[113] MRE 3:9.
[114] ME 1:11-12.
[115] Meam Loez 1:12.

In a gender war the battles are vicious. A tact oft employed is to secure a superior position through insult and humiliation. But the injured party invariably takes revenge for a back-facing ego is hyper-reactive to narcissistic wounds. The conflict escalates with invectives and recriminations.

The king became very angry [at Vashti's insubordination], and his anger burned inside him.[116]

Ramchal depicts a back-to-back relationship as two people speaking *at* each other, both talking at the same time.[117] Each demands the center-stage of the other's world. A narcissist views everyone as a mere extension of himself. Just as his own body obeys his will without a peep of resistance, so must others conform pronto to his every command. To voice a contrary will is to declare independence which (for back-to-backers) is an act of war. The narcissist is humiliated by this insubordination. He throws a tantrum, a day of rage.

And Memucan (aka Haman) answered in the presence of the king and the princes: "Vashti, the queen, has wronged not only the king, but all the princes and people in all the provinces...for now, all the women throughout the kingdom shall

---

[116] ME1:12.

[117] רמח"ל – קלח פתחי חכמה – 135.

despise their husbands when they hear that king Achashverosh commanded Vashti the queen to be brought to his presence, but she came not."[118]

Conflict management requires a level of maturity and self-awareness that is lacking in the chronically self-absorbed. Instead of stepping back and viewing the insult from a larger perspective that shrinks its significance, the narcissist does the opposite. The insult may be minor but he turns it into a blazing symbol of shame that undermines his entire sense of self-worth. The slightest affront gets magnified to exponential proportions. With Haman's input, Achashverosh's marital spat escalates into a world war.

[At Haman's advice] letters were sent to all the king's provinces…that every man should rule in his own house…[119]

This move to consolidate male power and to forcefully assert the right of husbands to rule over their wives, is viewed with disdain by the sages of Israel. "*R. Huna said: 'This decree of Achashverosh was utterly ridiculous. If a man wants to eat lentils and his wife wants to eat beans, can he force her? Surely she*

---

[118] ME 1:16-17.
[119] ME1:12.

does as she likes'.[120]A back-to-back relationship is about power and coercion. The wife is not respected as a free-standing individual with a will of her own. Decisions are not negotiated they are unilaterally decreed. The Book of Esther depicts this chauvinistic battle-cry in a most unfavorable light. A front-facing man does not need (or want) to rule over his wife. The reflex to invoke male privilege is a sure sign that a relationship is back to back. Haman's ideal of marriage is not a role model for the Jewish people.

And Haman said to King Achashverosh, There is one…(ישנו…אחד).[121]

> **ישנו … אחד can be literally read as the One (i.e., the God of Israel) is asleep (or at least appears to be so in relation to his people). … Said the Holy One, blessed be He… I will awaken from [the semblance of] sleep and protect my nation by smiting those who attempt to destroy them.[122]**

The surgical uncoupling of Phase 2 happens while the male partner is asleep, [123] as seen in its biblical

---

[120] MRE 4:12.

[121] Esther 3:7-8

[122] MRE 7:12

[123] האריי״זל עץ חיים – שער מעות הירח א׳.

prototype, "And the Lord God made *Adam* fall into a deep sleep, and he slept; and He took one of his sides, and closed up the flesh. And from the side which the Lord God had taken from *Adam*, He made woman…" In the Jewish tradition Israel and HaShem are beloved soul-mates. And so, in the Purim story, the sages note that when the time for uncoupling arrived, *HaShem*, true to His role, was (apparently) asleep.

"And the word pleased the king."[124] He gave the order and they brought Vashti's head in on a platter.[125]

The graph above shows that the surgical uncoupling of Phase 2 results in *woman*'s diminishment. Rav Ashlag explains that a spiritual curtain separates *woman* from her brains.[126] The condition of being estranged from one's intellect is a diminished state, at least according to Kabbala. Certainly, one loses a good foot-and-a-half if the head goes. It's a "shortened" stature. In real life it seems that *nesira* occurs in women's childbearing

---

[124] Esther 1:21.

[125] MRE 4:11.

[126] Rav Yehuda Ashlag, *HaSulam*, commentary on Zohar 3:157a; KW p. 99-135, **124**.

years.[127] Women often report, at this time, that their minds have turned to mush and that they've lost touch with their brains.

The head symbolizes a goal-directed approach to life. Removing the "head" creates a circle, a figure which has no beginning or end. It has no "head." And so it is often true that women's lives during this time are more circular in their rhythm. Changing diapers, the diapers get dirty, changing them again…washing dishes, the dishes get dirty, washing them again…cooking food, the food gets eaten, cooking again… For these and other reasons it seems that *woman*'s kabbalistic diminishment coincides with her childbearing years. Vashti's beheading is a crude (and literal) depiction of the spiritual surgery which Kabbala calls *nesira*.

Note: The term diminishment only applies to one isolated feature of this dramatic interval in woman's *life. It does not consider other fronts of growth that are blossoming at this very same time. It does not measure the deepening of heart, the sharpening of intuition, the building of character and the cultivating of generosity*

---

[127] In trying to relate this graph to real life, there are many clues suggesting that "diminishment" coincides with the period in women's lives when they are most intensely involved in their child bearing and child rearing responsibilities. Only one of these hints is mentioned here.

that simultaneously occur. From woman's *perspective the same period that Kabbala calls diminishment is in fact a growth spurt.*

And he brought up Hadassah, that is, Esther, his uncle's daughter; for she had neither father nor mother… and Mordechai adopted her as a daughter.[128] Once when he could not find a wet nurse, Mordechai's breasts actually produced milk to feed her.[129]

> **Don't read daughter (בת), read house (בית). This means that Mordechai took her as a wife (for a man's wife is his shelter).[130]**

In the kabbalistic model after the *nesira, woman* loses her direct access to the flow of light and consciousness that descends from the cosmic wellsprings. Instead, these lights are transferred to her *man* and it becomes his job to pass them to her. In the Ari's own words:

> *"Woman*'s path of development is different from *man*'s and she needs him to facilitate her passage. When *mother* raised *man* she designated a special energy fund earmarked for

---

[128] Esther 2:7.

[129] BR 30:8.

[130] TB, Meg. 12b.

woman's growth. This too, she transferred into *man*'s possession and he became its trustee. He serves as an intermediary between *mother* and *woman* and passes these special resources on to *woman*, thereby enabling her development. With his help she too evolves into a full stature of ten sefirot."[131]

When the king's decree was publicized, and the young girls were gathered …Esther was taken to the palace…[132]

Mordechai realized that he could not hide Esther forever…Mordechai escorted Esther to the public square where the women gathered to be brought to the king.[133]

The Purim story now depicts the step-by-step journey of Phase 3 where *woman* moves toward fullness of stature. This shifting of gender relations is not supposed to be a war, but a mutually welcomed and shared project. *Man*'s role is to build *woman* up by generously providing her with the

---

[131] KW, p.70. האריז״ל - ספר עץ חיים - שער מעוט הירח – פרק א׳
ואמנם גידול המלכות אינה אלא ע״י אמצעית ז״א עצמו, כי אמא עלאה
כאשר גדלה אותו, נתנה בו כח עוד גידול להמלכות. ואח״כ יצאה בחי׳
גידול זה של המלכות...גם כן, עד תכלית הגידול שבה, שהוא עד שתשלם
גם היא ליו״ס שלימות שבה.

[132] Esther 2:8.

[133] Manot HaLevi; Maamar Mordechai; Me'am Loez 2:8.

resources of lights and strengths that she needs to develop herself. The Ari identifies four milestones along the way. Each is defined as a positive step based on two criteria:

- *Woman*'s consciousness (and intellect) matures and expands, which metaphorically translates as spiritual height. The closer she comes to equality of stature with *man* the more perfected their union.

- The Ari then spotlights a particular by-product of this growth in stature which is *woman*'s dependency upon *man*, a condition that varies inversely with her "height." The "shorter" she is the more she relies upon him to fill the functions that she lacks. The "taller" she grows the more capabilities she incorporates into herself and consequently, the more self-sufficient she becomes. The ideal, says he, is for *woman* to become independent from *man* in this regard. Only without need can the couple unite from a love that is utterly free of ulterior motive. This is the Jewish vision of how *man* and *woman* will relate when they have healed themselves and fixed the world.

And so Mordechai "raises" Esther. He builds her up into a free-standing, independent woman and escorts her to the threshold, where Esther must now create her own autonomous relationship with the King, one that is no longer dependent on Mordechai's intervention.

The king loved Esther above all the other women for she found grace and favor in his eyes… and so he set the royal crown upon her head. Esther did not reveal her nationality or ancestry as Mordechai had charged her. Esther obeyed the command of Mordechai now, as when she was raised by him.[134]

Esther's relationship with the King is evolving. Now she has direct access, symbolized by her newly acquired crown which in Kabbala signifies the highest of the ten sefirot, the soul's superconscious link to HaShem. Yet still Esther looks to Mordechai as her guide. She remains in his tutelage, though soon she must forge her own independent channel of guidance straight from above.

Mordechai charged Esther…to approach the king…and supplicate for her people. *And Esther sent…a command to Mordechai*, "All the king's servants… know, that whoever…enters the king's inner court uninvited…will be put to death…*Then Mordechai commanded Esther*, "If you remain silent at this time …deliverance will come to the Jews in

---

[134] Esther 2:17-20

another way and you and your father's house shall be destroyed...". *Esther commanded Mordechai... "Gather together all the Jews of Shushan and fast for me...I too...will fast and then will I go to the king unbidden, though it is against the law..." Mordechai did according to all that Esther had commanded him.*[135]

In this exchange Esther comes into full stature. She and Mordechai function as equals. Their dialogue is perfectly symmetrical. They both command and they both obey. They solve their problem through negotiation. There is no power struggle between them.

And it came to pass on the third day, that Esther donned her royal dress and stood in the inner court of the king's palace opposite the king's chamber.[136]

Esther enwrapped herself in Divine inspiration (*ruach hakodesh*).[137]

This is Esther's initiation into a fully independent relationship with HaShem. She is on her own with no way to summon Mordechai's input. Alone with her instincts, she has to find God's holy word that

---

[135] Esther 4:8-17.

[136] Esther 5:1.

[137] TB Meg. 15a.

speaks through *them* as surely as He spoke at Sinai. At each step she scans the horizon for options, waiting for her heart to whisper yes and there she will move. An extended fast?...A wine-party for three?...Another? There are no neon signs or prophetic voices. This is trial by fire and the stakes could not be higher. Esther listened well and chose good. She saved her people and pulled the Oral Torah down into the hearts of the nation.

On that day King Achashverosh gave the estate of Haman, the Jew-hater, to Esther the queen. "Mordechai came before the king, for Esther explained who [Mordechai] was to her... And Esther set Mordechai over the house of Haman.[138]

Rav Shneur Zalman of Liadi explores the Ari's culminating stage of feminine development and concludes that at its highest point a reversal of polarities occurs.[139] In all the preceding stages, *man* is taller than *woman* (even if only a hair's breadth), and she needs him to pull down the lights that she cannot yet reach. But at the highest edge of the highest stage this polarity inverts. Like a spring compressed and released, the feminine's

---

[138] Esther 8:1-2

[139] KW, p. 225-268, **257**; -138 ר׳ שניאור זלמן – תפילת לכל השנה 139.

diminishment (in Phase 2) sets in motion a chain of events which propels her beyond her starting point (the initial equality of Phase 1, and the current crown of *man*'s stature). In Rav Shneur Zalman's own words:

> "In the future, this crown of superconscious lights that *man* received from *mother* will instead come from *woman* [i.e., his *wife*]. She, who had previously been below him in stature, will now surpass him and their roles will reverse. She will be holding their higher lights and he will receive his portion from her."[140]

And so here now, Esther is the one with greater access to the King and Mordechai gains entry via her queenly connections as the verse states, *"Mordechai came before the king, for Esther explained who [Mordechai] was to her."* Esther also now becomes a source of superconscious flow for Mordechai. She pulls the lights from above (i.e., from the King) and transfers them to Mordechai, as the verse explicitly states: *"King Achashverosh gave*

---

[140] אבל הנה לעתיד כתיב אשת חיל עטרת בעלה הרי בחי' מ"ל שנק' אשת חיל תהיה עטרת לבעלה שהוא ז"א ונמצא בחי' העטרה שעטרה לו אמו ביום חתונתו בזמן מ"ת הנה לעתיד יבא לו העטרה זאת דוקא מבחי' מלכות הנק' מקבל מפני שאור המלכות תתעלה אז למעלה מעלה מבחי' ז"א לפי שנעוץ סופן בתחליתן כי סוף מעשה דוקא עלה במחשבה תחלה וכמ"ש ביאור דבר זה במ"א באריכות.

Haman's estate to Esther the queen… And Esther set Mordechai over Haman's property."

Then Esther the queen, the daughter of Avichail and Mordechai the Jew, wrote with all authority… And the decree of Esther confirmed these matters of Purim; and it was written in the book.[141]

Esther wrote the sages that they should make the Megilla an authoritative text to be read on Purim as a permanent obligation and that it should be written like a Torah scroll. The sages refused for two reasons: 1) They feared the story would provoke a backlash of anti-Semitism and 2) The Torah forbids adding new commands and/or layers of Scripture beyond the original three (Torah, Prophets, and Writings).[142]

Esther convinced them to fulfill her request. She explained that writing the story of how the Jews defeated the Hamanites actually fulfilled the positive command (#189) "to remember the nefarious deeds of the Amalekites" (Exodus 17:14). When the Torah states this obligation "to remember," it

---

[141] Esther 9:29-32.

[142] TB Meg. 7a, which brings Mishlei 22:20.

continues with a further request to: "Write it in a book" (Exodus 17:14). Esther argued that the Megilla was simply fulfilling the Torah's command "to remember…and to write…" (since Haman was an Amalekite and the Megilla reminds us of his "nefarious deeds)." Since both the writing and the reading of the Megilla were Torah directives, argued Esther, the sages were not free to compromise based on what the gentiles might think and there was no worry that a *mitzvah* was being added to the Torah. The sages concurred and also attested that the Book of Esther was written with prophetic inspiration[143]. [144]

Esther and Mordechai wrote the Megilla together but Esther's name is mentioned first, for her contribution was more essential than his. The parts that she added turned the historical chronicle into an eternally relevant teaching tale.[145]

---

[143] Me'am Loez 9:29

[144] TB, Meg. 7a; [Yerushalmi, Megilla 1:5], Tirath Kesef (Salonika, 1736) by R. chaim Avraham Gatigno; Me'am Loez 9:29.

[145] פירוש האלשיך ז״ל - משאת משה על אסתר - פרק ט פסוק כט

...לזה אמר, דע איפה כי גם שמרדכי לא עשה עיקר מסיפור המגילה ולא כתב רק מאיש יהודי כמו שכתבנו על פסוק ויכתוב מרדכי את הדברים

Esther further became a source of light and influence (משפיע) to the sages of Israel. She presented a halachic proof that convinced the Sanhedrin to enshrine the Purim story as an official holiday that would be observed by the Jews of every generation forever more.

And it is this festival, Esther's holiday, that is the only one we will continue to celebrate in the World to Come.[146] The messianic and post-messianic bliss is nothing but the pleasure of *man* and *woman* finally meeting "face to face, core to core, cell to cell." Yet this can only be when they have finally grown "completely equal."[147]

If only we could integrate this truth into our bones: The rising of the feminine is a win-win situation. Its consummate union of equals is everyone's joy. This perfect marriage has been our (perhaps unconscious)

האלה, אך אחרי כן ותכתב אסתר את כל תוקף, הוא כל מיני תוקף המלך, שהוא מויהי בימי אחשורוש עד איש יהודי, כי שם יש מיני תוקף רבים כאשר הזכרנו. וזהו רבוי האת ורבוי הכל. וזאת עשתה אסתר והסכים עמה גם מרדכי. וזהו שלא נאמר ויכתבו אסתר וכי' ומרדכי וכי', וגם הקדים הכתוב את אסתר למרדכי מה שלא עשה כן בפסוק שאחר זה כי אם הקדים את מרדכי. אך הוא כי בזה היא התעוררה בדבר בעצם בראשונה, ואחריה מרדכי נמשך, וזהו ותכתב אסתר המלכה בת אביחיל ומרדכי היהודי את כל תקף:

[146] Yerushalmi Megila, chapter 1; *Yad*, end of Megilla.

[147] Ari, *Aytz Chaim, Hechal Nukva, Shaar Miut Ha Yareach*, ch.1; Schneider, KW, pp.52-98.

yearning for six thousand years, and from its realization flows all the promised blessings of the world to come.

Let it be that on this holy Purim fest, when the lights of Esther's crown stream through the world, that we "taste and know"—if just for that precious moment— how sweet it is to meet our Maker, Master and Cosmic Soul-mate Face-to-face and Core-to-core. And may the feminine in all her myriad guises be cleansed, honored, heartened and redeemed by that light. And may the masculine, with all his blessed strength, roll up his sleeves and get to work raising the feminine, inside and out, for that's the only way to bring Mashiach NOW.

A Purim Mantra in Haiku, 2008

Anything truly
Good for one is always sure
To be good for all.

PurimBurst, 2008/ 5568

(based on *Pri Tsadik*,[148] *Ohev Yisrael*[149]
and *Heichal HaBrocha*[150])

"Let the king and Haman come to the banquet."[151] The
Talmud asks, "Why did Esther honor Haman with an
exclusive invite to this tête-à-tête between her and the
king?" ... R. Joshua answers: She learned this strategy
(encapsulated by a verse from Proverbs) in her father's
house: 'If your enemy is hungry, give him bread to eat
and if thirsty ply him with drink. For in so doing you

---

[148] R. Tsadok HaKohen, *Pri Tsadik*, Purim 2 (part 2).

[149] R. Avraham Yehoshua Heshel, *Ohev Yisrael*, Parshat Zachor 1.

[150] R. Y.Y. Y. Safrin (the Komarna Rebbe), *Netiv Mitzvotecha,
netiv hayichud, shvil* 6, *ot* 3-5. This material is the subject of
Sarah [Yehudit] Schneider's book : *You Are What You Hate—A
Spiritually Productive Approach To Enemies.*

[151] Esther 5:4. This is also the one place in the Megilla where
the letters of God's essential name appear in their proper
order as the acronym of the four Hebrew words (יבוא המלך
והמן היום), "...let the king and Haman come today..."

heap coals of fire upon his head, and...God will cause him to make peace with you.'" [152,153]

Haman was a ruthless foe with genocidal aims. His cunning scheme to destroy all Jews was a first in Jewish history. Yet the ease with which Esther averted his menace—no bribes, no lives, no collateral damage—was equally unsurpassed.[154] How did she execute that turnabout? Is there a lesson that we can apply to parry *our* enemies with equal grace?

The Talmud says yes! Esther preserved her family tradition and heeded its cautions well. R. Tsadok HaKohen explains what this means. Esther,

---

[152] Proverbs 25:21.

[153] TB, Megilla 15b and Ein Yakov there.

[154] The real turnabout occurred with Haman's defeat. The subsequent war was a *fait accompli*. Mordechai and Esther's new decree only permitted the Jews to kill those who took up arms and attacked them despite the king's obvious change of heart. Haman's original decree functioned as a "strange attractor." It drew the hate mongers out from the pack, those who could not control their bloodlust. The gate now opened, the fantasy let loose, there were those who could not hold themselves back. They alone were slain by the Jews on that fateful pre-Purim day.

we're told was Mordechai's niece[155] and Mordechai hailed from Binyamin,[156] a pugnacious tribe[157] whose quarrelsome ways nearly caused it to go extinct.[158] A remnant was spared but their reprieve was conditional: the survivors must learn to sublimate aggression, for their next provocation would bring certain demise. Threat of extinction is a strong motive to change. The tribe of Binyamin learned to "make peace, not war"—to accomplish their aims by more skillful means. This is the legacy that guided Esther as she prepared to face off with Haman, the kingpin of Amalek in those days when Persia (now Iran) ruled the world.

Now every virtue requires the wisdom of temperance to employ its golden rule. Damage comes from both over-using or under-applying its holy (but relative) truth. Just as a sailboat does not face into the wind but tacks to the right and then to the left and then to the right again, so is this true for inner work. We hold an ideal but overshoot the mark and then back off (a bit too

---

[155] Esther 2:7. The Midrash elaborates that Mordechai's father hailed from Binyamin while his mother's roots were Yehuda.

[156] Esther 2:5.

[157] Judges 3:15-21; Judges 20:16; 1 Chronicles 12:2; 1 Chronicles 8:40 ; 2 Chronicles 14:7.

[158] Judges 19-21.

much) and then exert again. The zigs and zags become more subtle but do not disappear. The Midrash reports that the clansmen of Binyamin followed this tack when they metamorphosed from warriors into diplomats. Their guiding motto was encapsulated by King Solomon generations further on, "If your enemy is hungry, give him bread to eat and if thirsty ply him with drink. For in so doing you heap coals of fire upon his head and...God will cause him to make peace with you."[159] The tribesmen of Binyamin reinvented themselves, though their change would only endure if they could find their dignity inside this new path—if they discovered even sweeter wins than the glory of military triumph. Yet, they would have to cultivate their inner senses to access these new and more subtle delights—pleasures (infinitely more precious and stable) that lie beneath the surface on the inner planes.

The tribe of Binyamin learned to relish these wholesome and elusive joys—to take true delight in holy things like good and light and

---

[159] Proverbs 25:21.

consciousness. Binyamin's worldview completely transformed when it stretched to include the inner planes. A whole new set of factors appeared that—when incorporated into their cost-benefit analysis—changed its verdict and the life-decisions that were based upon it. The tribe of Binyamin looked *in* and *up* and this is what they found:

The entirety of creation is a single universe-encompassing *Adam* that spans from heaven to earth and includes the entire cosmos within its fuzzy bounds. The manufacturing method that HaShem employed to bring forth this *Adam*—as an autonomous creature distinguished by its capacity for free choice—entailed a chaotic interval of history called the "breaking of the vessels" when HaShem created and destroyed seven worlds[160].

The shards of these seven shattered kingdoms are called sparks and they are the raw materials out of which our world is built. They were injured, darkened and dirtied by their ordeal. Every spark must be cleaned, repaired, raised and actualized. Now we are a work in progress. The Messianic Era is nothing but the completion of this spark-raising effort.

---

[160] See under "Seven Worlds" in the glossary.

Some of these sparks are already raised and integrated into the physical, emotional, mental and spiritual planes of our world. These comprise the conscious layers of *Adam*. Some of these sparks continue to lie shattered in the dark invisible abyss which constitutes the unconscious layer of *Adam*'s universe-encompassing soul.

The universe is holographic which means that *Adam*'s structure repeats itself on every scale. Each individual soul (which is a cell in the cosmic Adam) also contains conscious layers (consisting of sparks that have already been rescued) and unconscious layers (which are sparks connected to its soul-cell that are yet to be raised).

These unactualized (subconscious) sparks are strewn throughout the universe. Wherever they lie they always remain linked back to their true root and will eventually return there when the time comes for them to be raised. Until then, these still-fallen sparks are likely to be temporarily lodged within the soul of someone (or something) else. Everything contains a mixture of sparks that truly belongs to it and sparks that belong to others which must eventually be returned to their true owners.

The only thing that will ultimately make us happy is to collect all the scattered sparks of our soul and finally become whole. The still-fallen-sparks connected to our soul are not yet part of our conscious self. They appear as not-us for they lie outside the confines of our self-image. The most fallen and estranged of them can even appear as an enemy who is so extremely not-us that he is actually trying to harm us.

An enemy holds an alienated spark connected to our soul that was severely disfigured in the primordial breaking of vessels and that we no longer recognize as a piece of our very own self. In its wounded condition this disowned sliver of fallen light lacks vision and emotional intelligence. Yet on a primal level it has chosen us as its opponent because it is trying, in its deluded way, to connect back to its root which really is us.

The sparks of ourselves inside the enemy must be recovered. It is critical to our well-being and we cannot finish with this world until we get them. The enemy is performing a service by bringing these lost sparks to our attention although his methods may be hurtful and unscrupulous.

The question becomes: How do we both protect ourselves and reclaim our sparks? What is the most spiritually productive way to succeed at this paradoxical mission? That is the task that Esther faced and she sought the counsel of her ancestral line. The tribesmen of Binyamin became as tenacious in their spark collecting as they had been stiff-necked in their warfare.

King Sha'ul (a Binyamite and Esther's holy forebear)[161] carried this family motto inside his heart as he waged his war with Amalek. But it was not the time for that, HaShem had made it clear. There is one enemy so fearsome and irredeemable that all compassion for him is misplaced. Amalek will exploit any glimmer of benevolence to advance its godless cause. Sha'ul lost his inner balance and veered to the side of mercy—his compassion overruled HaShem's explicit will and he let King Agag live. Rav Tsadok explains Sha'ul's lapse of judgment as a consuming concern for the holy spark of R. Shmuel ben Shilat (a tsadik and Talmudic giant) that was trapped inside King Agag's soul. How could Sha'ul not risk his crown to save this precious cargo? Haman's lineage was conceived the very night he was spared[162] and the spark of R. Shmuel bar Shilat, now saved from extinction, passed with Agag's seed to the great

---

[161] *Targum Sheni* (Quoted by Shlomo Alkabez, *Menot Halevi* [Venice, 1512]).

[162] The Talmud explains that Sha'ul not only spared King Agag's life but honored his royal status by allowing him conjugal visits.

great grandfather of wicked Haman whose soul touched ground that fateful eve.

Now, five hundred years later in the Purim story, these two pedigrees again converge: Esther, a descendent of Sha'ul (king of the Jews) meets Haman, a descendent of Agag (king of the Amalakites).[163] And Esther follows her family precedent but this time for good. Haman, chancellor to the king, promulgated a royal edict that on a certain date, nearly a year away, the populous can annihilate its Jewish neighbors. The king did not realize that he sentenced his beloved Queen Esther to death when he signed this decree. Esther's job was to plead for her people—to reverse the edict and secure amnesty.

Wrapped in light, clothed with Divine inspiration, Esther entered the king's chambers unbidden, an act that carried certain death unless his majesty showed mercy. The king's heart softened—he extended his scepter and allowed Esther to live. "What are you seeking my queen? Ask for anything—up to half the kingdom—and it is yours."[164] Esther, alone with her instincts, had to find God's holy word that speaks through *them* as

---

[163] ibid.

[164] Esther 5:3.

surely as He spoke at Sinai. There were no neon signs or prophetic voices (or even a battle plan). She cleaved to the wisdom of her family line and applied its guiding truth:

> If your enemy is hungry, give him bread to eat and if thirsty ply him with drink. For in so doing you heap coals of fire upon his head and...God will cause him to make peace with you.

"Let the king and Haman come this day to the wine banquet that I have prepared for him."[165]

Instead of requesting Haman's death right there on the spot (and losing any captive sparks trapped inside his wicked soul), Esther invited Haman *in*. R. Tsadok explains that Esther hoped (by her wine and grace) to arouse the spark of R. Shmuel bar Shilat that was locked inside Haman's soul. If she could revive that inner *tsadik* Haman might awaken to *teshuva*. Who knows what miracle HaShem would employ to redeem his holy nation. The turnabout could easily be for Haman to see the light, renounce his hatred and dedicate his life to God, good and truth.

Esther's plan actually worked...for a moment, says R. Tsadok. "Haman [left the banquet] that day

---

[165] Esther 5:4.

joyful and of good heart (שמח וטוב לב)."[166] Scripture does not employ that phrase (*good heart*) casually. It is an honorific term for joy that comes from tasting light (and truth). When referring to more material pleasures Scripture adds a qualifier and the phrase then reads, *a kind of good heart* (כטוב לב).[167] There is no qualifier here notes R. Tsadok. Esther kindled the holy spark and Haman awakened to *teshuva*…for real!

Yet when Haman left Esther's presence he could not sustain this awakening. His narcissistic tantrum resurged, triggered by Mordechai's refusal to bow. Haman lost his "good heart," his *teshuva* collapsed and the spark of R. Shmuel bar Shilat transferred to Mordechai via the channel of hatred directed toward him. And now without this holy spark to prop him up, to draw down life-juice and to shield him from the fallout of his evil ways Haman plummeted to his demise.

In the twenty-four hours following Esther's invite: Haman did *teshuva*, regressed, lost his holy spark to Mordechai, planned Mordechai's execution, had the gallows made, came for the king's permission to conduct the hanging *today*,

---

[166] Esther 5:9.

[167] Esther 1:10.

instead received the job of saluting Mordechai by leading him through the city streets and publicly proclaiming his praise, was rushed to Esther's second tête-à-tête, was exposed for plotting the queen's demise, fell on top of Esther, and was executed on the very gallows he had built for Mordechai. This dramatic tumble was catalyzed by Esther's wine party for it awakened a glimmer of *teshuva* in Haman which threw him off-balance and precipitated his downfall.

> Rebbe Akiva roused his dozing students with a curious remark: By what merit did Esther rule over 127 provinces? Because her ancestor, Sarah the matriarch, lived for 127 years.[168]

Sarah and Esther dealt with threats to Jewish survival in very different ways. When Sarah witnessed Ishmael endangering Isaac's life she pushed him faraway. When Esther confronted Haman's genocidal menace she invited him to the party. Ishmael remained an antagonist, while Haman self-destructed.

The Ohev Yisrael explains that when evil rises above its station it destabilizes and like a helium balloon it bursts and disintegrates. Esther invited Haman up into the inner chamber, into the private

---

[168] MR Gen. 58:3

banquet between herself and the King. In this rarified atmosphere (where only truth shines) the hostage spark quickens while its captor's illusion of legitimacy crumbles and a reversal occurs. The spark overpowers its abductor and their power relations invert. If the captor does *teshuva* the spark will bring him along—he will go through changes but he will be redeemed. If the captor does not accept this reversal and attempts instead to domineer, the spark will break loose and the captor, now bereft of the spark's merit (and protexia) will tumble to his demise.

How does Esther's model apply to us? The Ohev Yisrael explains that our mind has an inner chamber, called *chokhma*, where only truth resides. It is the place where conceptions and opinions deconstruct, reduce to their elementals, get flushed of impurities, rectify and emerge clean. Lies and illusions cannot survive in *chokhma*'s rarefied air (בחכמה אתבריה).[169] *Chohkma* is also the place of memory, says he. To recall the travesty of

---

[169] Zohar 2:254b; R. Isaac Luria (Ari), *Aytz Chaim*, 8:5 (and throughout his writings 35 times).

Amalek (as the Torah commands)[170] is the same as inviting Haman to a private banquet prepared in the inner chamber for ourselves and the King.

The Hebrew letters that comprise the term *chokhma* (חכמה) break down into two smaller words (כח מה), the "power of what," meaning the power of knowing that you don't know. To invite your enemy into *chokhma* is to invite him into the place of wonder, above judgment, where there are only questions: Why did HaShem create this enemy? Why did HaShem bring him into my life? How do I reconcile my faith in God's unswerving goodness with the brutality and injustice He allows in His world? How does HaShem want me to respond to this antagonist? What lessons am I supposed to learn? Are there captive sparks that can (and must) be rescued from this foe? What is the most efficient and least painful way to redeem what I can redeem and be rid of the rest...for good?

> The state of consciousness that enables this perspective is called "lots," i.e., literally *purim*. One goes deeply inward (and upward) to find a place inside that transcends craving and aversion. One's love-bond to God gets so deep,

---

[170] Dev. 25:17.

one's vision so vast, that the truest (and normally hidden) truth becomes real: Every moment is an opportunity for closeness with God and it is not clear which builds intimacy more, the joy or the pain, the blessing or the curse, Mordechai or Haman. Would there be Purim without Haman? Who do we thank more for this day?[171]

Esther had two paradoxical goals and refused to compromise either one:

1) She insisted on extricating the soul-spark of R. Shmuel bar Shilat (and any other holy sparks trapped inside her Amalekite foe).[172]

2) She sought to disarm (and ultimately eliminate) the murderous enemy who was plotting genocide against the Jewish people, as the Torah commands:

"...You shall blot out the memory of Amalek from under the heavens; you shall not forget."[173]

Esther accomplished her objectives without resorting to force.

---

[171]Sarah [Yehudit] Schneider, *PurimBursts*, pp. 21-25.

[172] Heichal HaBrocha in *Ketem Ofir*, 7:1, suggests that there was more than one spark in Haman, the Amalekite.

[173] Deut. 25:19.

A helium balloon stays stable because the atmosphere exerts pressure from the outside that matches the pressure within. But when the balloon rises, the atmosphere thins and the pressure from without no longer offsets the push from within. The balloon distends, destabilizes, pops and disintegrates...just like Haman.

The "pressure from within" is the narcissist's inflated sense of power and importance. The "pressure from without" is our judgments and conceptions of him. When, for a moment, we suspend all these certainties and enter a state of "knowing-that-we-don't-know" what is *really* happening here, the pressure changes and with

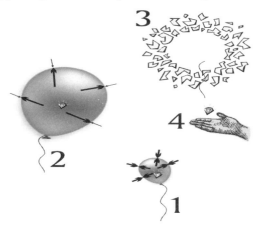

nothing to push against the narcissist's ego suddenly over-inflates, bursts and self-destructs.

As warriors the tribe of Binyamin learned to fight left-handed to surprise their enemies and throw them off balance.[174] Esther, true to her ancestry, applied exactly that strategy on the inner planes.

When we get stuck in our hatred the enemy toughens, says Heichal HaBrocha.[175] Esther tried something new. She invited the enemy up into the inner, holy chamber of *chokhma*, the place of wonder where certainty and judgment momentarily suspend. And there, suggests Heichal HaBrocha, she prayed for her enemy to do real *teshuva*—not a flimsy apology, but real, soul-transforming *teshuva*.[176] Esther, a shrewd strategist,

---

[174] Judges 3:15-21, Judges 20:16, 1 Chronicles 12:2.

[175] *Netiv Mitzvotecha*, *Netiv Hayichud*, *shvil* 6, *ot* 4-5.

[176] There is no free lunch in the universe. When a person does *teshuva* they must pay the full spiritual debt that they incurred from their wrongdoings. Their *teshuva* allows them to pay some portion of that debt through their remorse. To pray for someone's *teshuva* is not a request for them to be relieved of the measure-for-measure consequences of their deeds. It is simply asking that they realize the error of their ways, turn their lives to good and God and make their reparations in this world, now.

understood that this would yield the best possible outcome: The captive sparks of her own countrymen trapped inside her enemy's soul would be safely returned and the enemy itself would cease to be a danger, permanently, without need of a hyper-vigilant and massive army to avert future attacks.

And, according to Heichal HaBrocha, this prayer for the enemy's *teshuva* is a fail-safe tactic that cannot backfire. Either it achieves its aim by redeeming the spark and its enemy in tow or—if the enemy lacks all merit—that very prayer for his *teshuva* will (as we see with Haman) accelerate his demise. Either way the prayer for an enemy's *teshuva* will produce positive results for the one who speaks it (sincerely).[177]

If your enemy is hungry give him bread to eat: Invite the thought of him into the inner chamber of *chokhma*, the place of wonder and suspension of certainty. The place where a special bread is served (a quality of light) that nourishes truth and exposes lies. The temporary surrendering of judgment

---

[177] And really, the prayer for an enemy's *teshuva* produces the best possible outcome for *all* parties involved. It might be that the best thing for the evildoer (who is not going to do *teshuva*) is to self-destruct and in that way stop generating more spiritual debts which are very painful to repay.

breaks down the old form which expels impurities and allows the elements to rearrange into a new (and hopefully more rectified) structure. In the shorthand of Kabbala:

(78 = מזלא = לחם = החכמה).[178]

If he is thirsty give him water to drink: Pray for the holy sparks trapped inside this evildoer. Pray that they find the strength to rise and shine and awaken the enemy himself to a true and complete *teshuva*. "Pour out your heart like water in the Presence of God...for the life of your young children [the unborn sparks, like Shmuel ben Shilat, that are trapped in the *other side*], who are faint from famine [from scarcity of light and truth and love and all things holy]..."[179]

For in so doing you heap coals of fire upon his head: A *teshuva* process almost always entails some fiery purgation. Perhaps it is the burning shame a person feels for their past misdeeds or perhaps the sufferings of life. Either way these purgations cleanse the soul and facilitate (possibly even initiate) the *teshuva*.

---

[178] Those versed in kabbalistic lore will grasp the significance of the equation.

[179] Lamentations 3:19.

And HaShem will cause him to make peace with you: Either because he transforms into a true ally or self-destructs.

Let it be, on this very Purim day, as we reenact Esther's wine party (on both the outer and the inner planes), that we access the place above knowing—the Chamber of Knowing-That-We-Don't-Know (עדל״יא) which is open to the public on Purim—and as we stand inside that holy inner recess, let us remember our enemies and pray for their complete and total teshuva exactly as we pray for our own three times daily. [180]And the power of our collective prayer echoing from that inner sanctum should catalyze the cosmic turnabout—sparks should rise, evil should disintegrate and Mashiach should appear, NOW.

---

[180] *Heichal HaBrocha* 5:4.

PurimBurst, 2009 / 5569

Esther inspired affection in the eyes of all who saw
her… (Esther 2:15)

What was the secret of Esther's extraordinary
(even supernatural) grace?[181] It wasn't her
sense of fashion, for she did not primp even before

---

[181] A compendium of passages which describe Esther's grace:
**"Esther inspired affection in the eyes of all who saw
her…The king loved Esther more than all the other women**
he had met, one each night, in the four years since Vashti's
execution…**Esther awakened grace and inspired his favor so
he set the royal crown upon her head and made her
queen**…Esther agreed to plead that her people be spared
annihilation. She risked her life by entering the King's
chamber [uninvited], a forbidden act that carried the death
penalty…**Esther donned royalty,** slipped past the guards **and
stood in the inner court facing the King…When the king
noticed Queen Esther…she inspired his affection."**

her first big night with the king.[182] And it wasn't her physical features, as captivating as they were,[183] for outer beauty, though compelling, always has detractors—it inevitably, also, arouses envy. Not so for Esther who found grace in *everyone*'s eyes. Before she revealed her Jewish roots each nation was sure she was one of them.[184]

The Ya'arot D'evash[185] discloses her secret: *All those that Esther met saw themselves in her because she would see herself in them.*

> Esther inspired affection in all who met her because, even though she was the most powerful woman in the world, she related to every person as her equal. This was not a manipulative strategy but the truth of how she saw the world. Esther identified so deeply with the essence of people—all people—that they felt as if she was *their* soul-sister, cut from the same cloth, reared in the same household.

---

[182] Esther, 2:15.

[183] Esther Rabba 6:9:" ...Esther was like a masterpiece of art, a statue, whose beauty crosses all cultural bounds....Esther's beauty roused affection in heavenly and earthly beings, alike."

[184] TB Meg. 13a.

[185] R. Yehonaton Eibshitz (1690-1764), *Ya'arot D'vash*, *chelek* 1, *drush* 5.

Everyone felt seen, mirrored and drawn to Esther through a mysterious bond of reciprocal affection.

Every soul has a specialty. Each person brings some facet of Godliness into focus through the lens of his or her life. It may be the virtue that one values most or an area where one naturally excels. Sometimes it's glimpsed when one feels "in the zone," but it may be the place where one struggles most. Just as there is a uniform code of spiritual law articulated by the Torah, so do we each have a *special* assignment that is optional for others but binding on us. R. Isaac Luria (the Ari) teaches that we are obligated to strive toward perfection in the area of our soul specialty and if we don't it counts as a debit, no less than transgressing the uniform code.

Esther's specialty was her compassionate x-ray vision, the honor she showed toward all humanity. Wherever she looked she saw to the core, to the Godly spark embedded there. Esther was utterly dedicated to her people yet lacked all trace of racist taint. It is no surprise that this was her test, to perfect this virtue to an ultimate degree.

Everyone knows that Esther risked her life when she entered the king's chambers unbidden to beg that he retract the decree calling for her people's extinction. Yet in that fateful moment she risked more than death and was tested on many fronts.

When she passed through that door she forfeited all hope of resuming her marriage to Mordechai.[186] Initiating this tryst with the king would irrevocably seal her fate—she must remain forever, now, Ahashverosh's wife.

And still there was another test that stunned her at that doorway. The Talmud recounts:

Esther…stood in the inner court of the king's palace.[187] R. Levi comments on this verse: As Esther prepared to plead for her people, she reached the chamber of the *tslamim* [usually translated as idols] and felt the *Shekhina* leave her fallen and bereft of grace. Broken she cried out the words of Psalm 22, "My God, My God, why have You forsaken me?"[188] Continuing her conversation with God and seeking to know why the *Shekhina* had abandoned her, Esther speculates…Perhaps it is because I called Ahashverosh a 'dog', as the psalm reads further

---

[186] TB Meg. 13a.

[187] Esther 5:1

[188] Psalm 22:2.

on, "Deliver my soul from...the dog."[189] Straightaway she retracted her words and esteemed him with the title of lion as the psalm continues, "Save me from the lion's mouth."[190,191]

Even in this extreme situation, where the king designated Esther his wife without considering her consent (while in fact her heart belonged to her beloved Mordechai); and even after he crowned her as queen he continued to gather the virgins and he was in cahoots with Haman the Amalakite, archenemy of the Jewish nation, and had issued a decree for her beloved people's genocidal extinction--even with all these justifications (personal, national and religious) the *Shekhina* would not tolerate a disparaging word from Esther about this idolatrous tyrant.

The Talmud employs a term that does not appear in the Biblical tale: it describes Esther

---

[189] Psalm 22:21

[190] Psalm 22:22.

[191] Megilla 15b

ותעמד בחצר בית המלך הפנימית. אמר רבי לוי : כיון שהגיעה לבית הצלמים - נסתלקה הימנה שכינה, אמרה : (תהלים כ"ב) אלי אלי למה עזבתני, שמא אתה דן על שוגג כמזיד ועל אונס כרצון? או שמא על שקראתיו כלב, שנאמר (תהלים כ"ב) הצילה מחרב נפשי מיד כלב יחידתי. חזרה וקראתו אריה, שנאמר (תהלים כ"ב) הושיעני מפי אריה .

approaching the chamber of *tslamim,* plural of *tselem*, which means image and is assumed here to mean idols. The standard interpretation is that the Divine Presence does not dwell in a place of spiritual impurity and the presence of idols is the ultimate desecration. Since Ahashverosh was an idolater, there were sure to be idols in his throne-room and they are what caused the *Shekhina* to leave when Esther crossed that threshold.

Yet, there is another interpretation even more consistent with the original verse and with Esther's successful remedy. *Tselem* is the term the Bible employs to teach that we humans were "created in the *image* of God." The chamber of *tslamim* becomes the inner soul core of human beings where their spark of Godliness dwells. The verse that inspired the Talmud's commentary is thus accurately read: "Esther stood in the inner court of the [*heavenly*] King's palace [the chamber of *tslamim*, where the image of God resides.]." Esther's job, her Divine mission, was to never lose sight of the holy *tselem*, the image of God that dwells at the core of all who stood before her.

Only with Esther's humble grace can one enter the chamber of *tslamim* where a brief lapse of anger or a racist word counts as a full-fledged sin (evidenced by the *Shekhina's* retreat when she called Ahashverosh a dog). The Shem M'Shmuel notes that her insult equated him to Amalek, which closed all doors to his *teshuva* and transformation.[192] In contrast, a lion is the noblest of creatures, identified with Judah and one of the three holy beasts on the heavenly Throne of Glory.[193] To label him a lion is to affirm his holy root and the possibility (nay, inevitability) of his *teshuva*. That is the only viewpoint that is welcomed in the Holy of Holies where the image of God resides. Smuggle in a racist slur and the *Shekhina* drops you like a leaden idol.

But Esther held the paradox. She didn't turn her gracious heart into a rigid ideology that paralyzed her from employing might to defend her nation if necessary. She commandeered the war with Amalek as the text clearly states.[194] And she even made difficult decisions that increased enemy casualties. Yet her judgment was not skewed by rage or racist hatred. She designed the most

---

[192] Amalek is compared to a rabid dog in midrashic and later writings while the Jewish people are likened to lions, the noblest of beasts.

[193] The Throne of Glory had as its four supports: a lion, ox, eagle and man.

[194] Esther, chapters 8 and 9.

spiritually productive battle plan to assure her people's safety and she acted decisively.

It is painfully clear that our greatest challenge as a people is to heal the rifts among ourselves. But how? We study the laws of right-speech and try to refrain from slander. We commit ourselves to generous deeds and weave threads of love that way. Our prayers are for the Jewish nation including everyone. Yet all these seeds will only sprout if they fall on fertile soil. And for this (literally) ground-breaking work Esther is our model. Our fierce drive to heal our people must rest upon a universal base. We must cultivate a habit of kindness toward the peoples and creatures of the world.

In *Duties of the Heart*,[195] R. Bechaya brings a teaching tale:

> A group of students were walking with their rabbi along a country road. They passed the carcass of a rotting dog that wafted a foul odor. The disciples commented on how putrid the carcass smelled. The old sage answered them, "How white are its teeth!" The pupils immediately regretted their disparaging

---

[195]R. Bechaya, *Duties of the Heart* (Feldheim) Vol II: p. 99 (chapter 6, Humility)

remark. If it is reprehensible to make a derogatory comment concerning a dead dog, how much more so is it wrong to denigrate a living human being…The goal of this pious rabbi was to instill the habit of viewing the world with a kind eye, even something as lowly as a dead dog.

Ours is a holographic world, which means that every piece contains something of every other piece inside itself. And that means that every nation also embodies aspects of every other nation as well. And that means that if we cannot honor (even celebrate) the diversity of peoples, cultures and creatures on our planet then we will not succeed in "loving our holy Jewish brethren as ourselves," for when they remind us of a nation for which we feel contempt our love will fast dissolve into disdain.

Let it be that on this holy Purim day, when Esther's lights stream through the world, that they wash away our racist taints (individual and collective) so that we fix our gaze on the image of God in all the places it be found. And with Esther's twinkle in our eye, let us pass through all the barriers that block us from our King, and there, within that sanctum, standing face to face, let us pray that every word we speak and every act we do should always bring the greatest good that is possible at that time. And in that way, together all, we should bring Mashiach now. For if we follow Esther's lead and cleanse our hearts from pride our prayer is sure to draw down grace, for that's the promise of this day.

A fanciful afterthought: It is curious to note, that Ahashverosh was the king of Persia, which in 1935 changed its name to Iran (which means, Land of the Aryans) in order to affiliate with Hitler's master race (identified as Aryan for real or imagined reasons). Iran (the land of these self-indentified Aryans) has publicly stated its genocidal intention to wipe Israel off the map.

Historically, it appears that the Aryans were the original Brahmin caste in India that introduced the earliest scriptural writings, called the Vedas which Jewish tradition connects to the verse in Genesis 25:6. After Sarah died Abraham remarried Ketura (which commentaries identify with Hagar, the mother of Ishmael) and had six additional sons "to whom he gave gifts, and sent them…eastward, to the east country." Commentators note the similarity between A-braham and Brahman (as well as other commonalities) and speculate that the gifts Abraham sent with his sons were the mystical teachings that seeded early Brahmanism. Apparently the elite Brahman status was originally connected to the spiritual wisdom they possessed.

It is also interesting to note that the word Aryan, in Hebrew, actually means "lion-like", and that one-and-a-half thousand years before Esther honored Ahashverosh with the title of lion, Jacob

(Abraham's grandson) blessed his son Yehuda / Judah (the one whose name represents the entire Jewish people, who are called Yehudim, i.e., Jews) with the following words: "Young lion (arye), Judah, you have risen from prey, my son. He crouches like a lion, like an awesome lion, who will dare rouse him?"[196] In fact, an emblem among Jews almost as common as the Jewish Star is the Lion of Judah. It is a strange irony that these Aryans, who seem at least recently, to have such compelling hatred for the Jewish race might actually trace their leonine roots to Abraham, the first Jew.

---

[196] Translation from, Aryeh Kaplan, *The Living Torah*.

PurimBurst, 2010 / 5570

Inspired by *R. Tsadok HaKohen, Likutei Amarim, essay 5*

One is obligated to drink [wine] on Purim until one doesn't know the difference between cursing Haman and blessing Mordecai (*Shulchan Aruch* 695:2).

The Ari explains the *tikun* that happens through this peculiar *mitzvah*: In every fallen person or sinful moment there is a sliver of God that enables that opposer-of-good to exist for there is only one source of life and that is HaShem the One-and-Only-Sustainer-of-Worlds. Those poor slivers of God trapped within the sociopath are coerced to enliven his wayward deeds—even when he scorns all that God holds dear. The spark of life inside him is actually a chip off our very own block, a holy brother sequestered by the *other side*. The problem is how to send love to our comrade-spark without energizing its malevolent captor—how to keep the spark alight till its rescue can be arranged.

That, says the Ari, is the secret and power of Purim and in particular its *mitzvah* of inebriation.

When a person, in their drunken state, accidently blesses Haman (though he meant to bless Mordechai), he sends light to the holy spark trapped inside Haman [a symbol for the evil realms which includes all our enemies both inside and out]. Yet because the blessing was unconscious and accidental it does not empower the Amalakite, himself, only the spark that's held captive there. [And the stronger the spark the greater its might to tug the system toward the light—captor and all.].[197]

Most of the time an absent mind produces failure, fall and damage. "A *mitzvah* without intention is like a body without a soul."[198] The sages teach that witlessness is the cause of all

---

[197] *Pri Eitz Chayim*, Shaar Chanukha and Purim, Chapter 6

[198] Rabbi Yitzchak Luria (1534-15720, *Likutei Torah LeArizal*, "Parshaat Ekev" [in the beginning]; Rabbi Yeshaya Halevi Horowitz (1570-1630), *Shenei Luchot Habrit* (Jerusalem: 1965), Vol 1, p. 249b.

misdeeds. "No one sins except if a spirit of folly overcomes him for a moment". [199]

But, on Purim, the opposite is true. We actually cultivate folly—there is a certain *tikun* that only occurs when we suffer a lapse of awareness. Presence of mind is our perennial goal but on Purim we seek to escape it. The explanation is as follows:

In general, the power of a *mitzvah*'s *tikun* is in proportion to its mindfulness. A *mitzvah* performed by rote, accomplishes minimal advancement—a spark gets extracted but remains earthbound.[200] It lacks the wings of love and fear to carry it aloft. Like a precious stone mined from the earth and left lying on the ground the spark remains below. The more passion and intention one brings to that deed the higher the spark ascends. A *mitzvah* performed with lucid awareness—the selfless desire to serve good and delight God—that is the purest of motives and it brings the greatest *tikun*.[201]

But what happens to those earthbound sparks released but left behind when we perform a

---

[199] TB, Sota 3a

[200] See Sarah [Yehudit] Schneider, *Eating as Tikun*.

[201] *Tanya*, Chapter 39.

mitzvah by rote? Are they doomed to eternal limbo? The Ari says, No! As soon as we come back and perform that same *mitzvah* with greater intention or recite that prayer with concentration, this new service "pierces the firmament" and carries with it the sparks that could not rise on their own.

There is no wasted *mitzvah*. Even when we space out altogether and barely take advantage of the potential of the moment, spiritual work is done. The deed itself extracts the spark. And the next day or week or year or lifetime, when we come back and perform it again, this time with full *kavanna*, those previous sparks get lifted by these ones with greater oomph.

R. Tsadok extends this principle to the Passover Seder which is the only time of year that eating becomes a full-fledged *mitzvah*, meaning that we actually recite a blessing over that act of consumption: "Blessed are You HaShem...who has commended us to eat this *matzah* (or *maror* or, when relevant, *Korban Pesach*)." Eating thus becomes an act of holy service. And just as we learned about prayer—that a passage recited with soulful intent will uplift all the times it was spoken by rote—so does the Seder raise all the earthbound sparks produced by unconscious eating. These three moments of *mitzvah*-eating (the only three of the whole year) can even redeem a spark from food that was eaten with gluttonous intent as long as it was *kosher*. The Seder can raise our neutral deeds and wrong intentions but it cannot reverse the callousing of soul that comes from forbidden foods.

Yet that precisely is the power of Purim—it is the one day when folly itself becomes a *mitzvah*. And thus it can redeem all the foolish (and fallen) deeds that were performed throughout the year. The implications are profound for we have already learned that: "A person does not sin except when a spirit of folly overtakes him." When eating becomes a *mitzvah* it redeems our gluttonous consumption—when folly becomes a *mitzvah*, it raises our foolish deeds—a Talmudic euphemism for sins, as we have seen.

This explains Purim's legendary power to effect *teshuva* in a way that even surpasses the day that is specially designated for *teshuva*, our Day of Awe called Yom Kippur. Everyone knows the Ari's famous teaching based on the Hebrew words for Purim (פורים) and Yom Kippurim (יום כפורים); where the difference between them is simply the letter כ (which, as a prefix, means, "like" or "similar to."). This hints to the secret relationship between these two days where Yom Kippur becomes literally, the day that is כי (like) Purim. The Hebrew language thus ascribes the primary (and trend-setting) holiness to *Purim*. Yom Kippur strives for Purim's sanctity but never quite measures up. It comes close enough to be called, "like Purim," but never supersedes.

On Yom Kippur the reconciliation of our relationship with God is the fruit of *conscious* inner work—scrupulous confession, heartfelt apology and fierce commitment to change. On Yom Kippur the reward is in proportion to the effort. Our soul is cleansed from the flaws that we admit (and lament) on that awesome holy day.

Yet the grace of Purim extends to even our unconscious flaws—the sins we continue to deny—the still-fallen sparks connected to our soul that provide life-juice to the Hamans of the world (including our own narcissistic layers of self). The light of Yom Kippur does not penetrate that dark, outer edge of our psyche. Only Purim, with its *mitzvah* of inebriation, can enliven the sparks trapped within our blind spots without providing succor to the delusions that ensnare them.

Yet, says the Ari, this mission can only succeed if we relinquish conscious control and trust

HaShem to guide our instincts on this day of holy folly. When a person fulfills the *mitzvah* of drinking [wine] on Purim his ego lapses into a quasi-prophetic reverie (called *tardema*). Then the *pintila yid* takes the reins and we slip into the groove of un[self]conscious awareness (because the self, i.e. the ego, is anesthetized with wine). And it is here that the Purim *tikun* occurs. In this exalted state of Divinely-sanctioned folly, the subliminal wisdom of our primal self, for a moment leads the way and assures that we will "bless Haman" (mistakenly) on this irreverent holy day. And that blessing transmits life-juice to the captive sparks held there and converts them into born-again emissaries of the light.

The danger is if the ego is only faking sleep, and secretly exploits this unguarded moment to advance its hedonistic interests. In that case the nurture directed toward the holy sparks sequestered by the *other side* gets waylaid by their captors and the mission backfires. Instead of strengthening the sparks it fuels the narcissistic delusions that imprison them.

There are those who weigh the risks against the benefits of this mission and reckon that it isn't worth the gamble. Better to drink a little more than usual and go to sleep (literally) and fulfill the *mitzvah* that way, than take the chance you'll crash and burn and cause more harm than good. For slumber is another way of losing the distinction between cursing Haman and blessing Mordechai.[202]

One who chooses this latter option must remember, nonetheless:

> The obligation to drink more wine than usual on Purim is one of the specific *mitzvot* of Purim day and there are deep reasons and secrets for it. One who refrains from fulfilling this *mitzvah* because he doesn't understand it cuts himself off from the community of Israel and rebuffs the yoke of rabbinic authority.[203]

The *mitzvah* of "drinking to inebriation on Purim until you don't know the difference between blessing Mordechai and cursing Haman" is actually the spiritual equivalent of *matanot l'evyonim* (giving charity to the poor), another *mitzvah* that is specifically obligated on this day. Our holy sparks trapped by the *other side*—be they prisoners of war, prisoners of Zion, prisoners of addiction, prisoners of our own narcissism, prisoners of cults, prisoners of ignorance—these captive sparks are spiritually

---

[202] *Shulchan Aruch w/Mishnah Brurah* 695:2 MB5, *Kitzur Shulchan Aruch* 144:6, *Chayei Odom* 155:8, *Kaf Hachaim* sk16.

[203] *Bina L'ittim Drush 21, Nitay Gavriel* 73:1

impoverished and there is virtually no other way to get rejuvenating lights to them. Any resources directed their way get intercepted by their captors and that, sadly, causes more harm than good.

Purim is the one day of the year when these destitute sparks get filled to the brim with sweet, clean, invigorating lights…and there is no pilfering by the *other side*. And now, fortified by their Purim manot[204], these holy (but estranged) sparks get raised by our folly, awakened by our reverie (*tardema*), cleansed by the *mitzvah* and transformed from dispirited prisoners into missionaries of the light. What a great and holy deed is the *mitzvah* of inebriating on Purim.

Seize the moment! Bring *all* your sparks to the party (which only happens when your *whole* self comes along)[205] for that fulfills the Purim motto: NO SPARK LEFT BEHIND!

Let it be, HaShem, that as individuals, as members of the community of Israel and the larger world

---

[204] Literally, "portion" and hinting to another one of the mitzvoth obligated on Purim—the mitzvah of *Mishloach* **Manot** (giving food portions to friends).

[205] That's the whole point of Purim masks—they create the space for you to become even more fully yourself.

community, that we should, through our holy Purim festivities, draw a flow of joy and revealed good into the heart, bones, cells and spaces of your creation and of every creature in it. May our celebrations of eating, inebriating, dancing and learning be pleasing in Your eyes. Please guide and inspire our study that Your will and Your holy Torah's truths should fill our hearts and transform our lives in ways that are only good.

גל עיני ואביטה נפלאות מתורתך

Open my eyes and I will behold the wonders of your Torah.[206]

A Related Chassidic Story

During his stay in Mezritch, the Rav of Kolbishov saw an old man come to the Maggid and ask him to suggest a *tikun* that would wash away his sins. "Go home," said the Maggid. "Write all your sins down on a slip of paper and bring it to me." When the man brought his list, the Maggid glanced at it briefly and comforted him as follows: "Go home. All will be well." But later the Rav of Kolbishov observed the Maggid reread the list and laugh at every line. This strange behavior shocked the Rav and actually even annoyed him. "How could someone reputedly holy laugh at another's sins!"

For years he did not forget the incident and remained bothered by it. Then, one Shabbat, he heard someone quote a teaching from the Baal Shem Tov:

"Everyone knows the Talmudic dictum that 'no one commits a sin unless a spirit of folly overcomes him.' The Talmud is teaching us that a sinner is a fool. And if a sage encountered a fool who was spouting silly, childish tales and obvious delusions…would the sage take offense or try to reason with the man? Both would get him nowhere and might even make things worse. A better option would be to find the humor in his folly—

the silliness of his behavior given what he's hoping to accomplish, the short-sidedness of his strategy given how the world really works—and laugh with him at the absurdity of his predicament. And as he laughs, the defensiveness melts and a spirit of kindness wafts through the world. The fool's small-minded perspective softens, his horizons broaden and a vision of higher possibility illumines the moment."

As the Rav reflected on this teaching his heart opened: "Now I understand the laughter of the Maggid when he read that list of sins."

EAT, DRINK AND BE HOLY

Glossary

Activation Energy – In chemistry, it is the minimum amount of energy (usually heat) that must be added to the starting ingredients in order to initiate a reaction (which is the chemical term for transformation).

Adam and *Chava* (Adam and Eve) – The archetypal man and woman in the Bible's creation story. The original human being was created as a single body combining both male and female aspects who were, together, called *Adam*. Only later were these two halves separated into a man and woman. The souls of all humanity derive from this archetypal human being that spanned from the heavens to the earth.

Amalek - This is a Biblical nation, distinguished by its exceptional corruption, cruelty, and denial of God. Amalek has come to symbolize the deepest and irredeemable root of evil in the universe. All of evil's secondary manifestations will be cleaned and salvaged. Only Amalek has no portion in the world-to-come. In the Torah's lexicon of symbols Amalek becomes the token of pure evil.

Ari – R. Isaac Luria (1534–1572), called the Ari (literally lion) which is actually an acronym of his titles and name. Master kabbalist who integrated theprofuse body of Jewish mystical teachings that preceded him into a coherent metaphysical system that carries the full authority of Oral Torah. His comprehensive revelations are the foundation truths upon which all subsequent kabbalistic writings build.

Atika – The highest root of the soul. The innermost point of the *sefira* called *keter* (crown), which actually touches the Infinite Light and dwells in the pleasure and faith of that union. The deepest source of Divine influence that transcends reward and punishment, and lies beyond the range of prayer. The only way to access it, maybe, is through silence."

Ayin – See NoThing

Back-To-Back Relationship – An immature and self-absorbed mode of relating where neither partner ever really "sees" the other, except as an object whose sole purpose is to satisfy their narcissistic needs. Adam and Eve's relationship before their *nesira* was back-to-back.

Bible – There are twenty-four books in the Jewish Bible (called *Tanakh*). They include the Torah (5), the Prophets (8), and the Writings (11).

Chashmal – Literally, electricity or electrum. A word that appears in Ezekiel's vision that is comprised of two subwords: *chash* (which means silence) and *mal* (which means speech). It conveys the kabbalistic advice about how to work with paradox, which is to vibrate back and forth between the two mutually exclusive truths.

Chassidut, Chassidism – Literally, "piety" or "loving-kindness." The movement within Judaism founded by the Baal Shem Tov (1698–1760) which emphasizes unconditional love of the people, Israel, and the fact that God's Presence permeates all levels of reality. It uses the inner dimensions of Torah to awaken the Jewish people to their collective inner self, and in this way, seeks to usher in the messianic era. The term, *Chassidut*, is also used more generally to refer to an attribute or way of life that goes beyond the letter of the law.

Chesed – Acts of kindness and generosity to those in need. It is the fourth of the ten *sefirot*, designating the Divine attribute of kindness and benevolence.

Chokhma – The second *sefira*, translated as wisdom. The power of insight. The initial point where a thought is first conceived. It is the second of the ten *sefirot* when counting from *keter*.

Chutzpa – gall, boldness, audacity, impudence. Can be a positive or negative trait depending upon how it is used. There is definitely use for holy *chutzpa*.

Circle World - Phase Two of cosmic history where the *sefirot* emanated as ten concentric circles. This arrangement was originally unrectified. It shattered and our linear universe appeared in its place. The Circle World's non-hierarchical reality will eventually replace our own as the future ideal.

Commandments – see *mitzvot*.

Eden – Paradise. The term which describes the nature of physical reality before the "shattering" and fragmentation that followed Adam and Eve's sin. Eden is the condition where Hashem's presence visibly permeates reality, and all things are expressing their perfection and exist in a state of union with God.

Eighth Kingdom – Kabbala teaches that there were seven universes created and destroyed before our own, number eight in the sequence. These seven shattered worlds comprise the Era of Chaos while ours, the eighth, is the beginning of their repair. For this reason the Eighth Kingdom is called the Rectified World. This teaching is the mystical interpretation of Genesis 36:31-39 which describes seven kings that ruled and died and an eighth whose death is not mentioned. The name of the king who ruled the primordial eighth kingdom is Hadar and Kabbala identifies Hadar with the root of Moses' soul.

Eight Kings – See: Eighth Kingdom.

Evil – Literally broken or unstable. The illusion of existence as separate and independent from God.

Front-To-Front Relationship – A relationship of true and healthy love. The couple bonds from mutual desire and shared vision. This possibility of relationship only arises after *nesira*.

Gadlut – Literally, maturity. This a term used in Kabbala to indicate a broad and mature state of spiritual development.

Gehinnom – The cleansing and purgation that a soul must endure on the inner planes as a prerequisite to claiming its "plot" of eternity in the spiritual Garden of Eden in the World of Souls.

Gematria – Every Hebrew letter possesses a number value. The numerical total of the letter, word or phrase is called its *gematria*. When words or phrases have the same *gematria* they are understood to hold a special relationship to each other. Many secrets and meditations are based on the science of these equivalencies.

Gevurah – The fifth *sefira*, translated as might or justice, expresses itself in several ways. It meters the impulse to give forcing it to adapt to the vessel's capacity to receive; it negates all that which opposes the will of God and it is the boundary-making, form-building power within creation.

Gilgul – The Hebrew term for reincarnation. The parts of the soul that were not cleansed and actualized in a previous lifetime must come back into one or several new lives to complete their work. Any portion of the soul that was cleaned and actualized in the course of that original lifetime does not come back but rather enters the lower Garden of Eden (on the inner planes called the World of Souls).

God – A simple, working definition is derived from the four-letter, essential name of God, which is built from all the permutations of the verb "to be." It thus translates as THAT WHICH WAS, IS AND WILL ALWAYS BE. God is beyond gender, containing both male and female elements as well as levels of oneness where even the duality of gender does not exist.

Haiku – An unrhymed Japanese poem having three lines of five, seven and five syllables each.

Halacha – Literally, walking. The vast system of Jewish law derived from the Torah as received by Moses and explicated by the sages which defines the entirety of Jewish life. There is no area of experience that is outside the jurisdiction of *halacha*.

HaShem – Literally, The Name. It refers to God in general, though it specifically indicates the unutterable name (or Tetragrammaton) which emphasizes the transcendent, eternal and compassionate attributes of God.

Holographic System – A holographic system is one where every sub-part contains information about the whole and every other sub-part within itself. Consequently, in a holographic system, it is possible to reconstruct the entire structure from any insolated component.

Holy of Holies – The portable desert Tabernacle that accompanied the Israelites in the forty-year desert journey had outer and inner chambers that reflected the degree of Divine revelation there. This is also true for the Temple in Jerusalem which replaced it. The Holy of Holies is the innermost chamber where only the holiest person (the High Priest) could enter on the holiest day of the year (Yom Kippur).

I-center – A point of consciousness that experiences the world with itself at the center. A perspective on the world that is both unique (because no one else sees it quite that way) and distorted (because vast swathes of reality lie outside its visual field).

Infinite Light or Infinite One – God's transcendent and primordial revelation. His simple, radiant, infinitely powerful light. The contraction which initiated the creative process caused this Infinite Light to become hidden within the circumscribed area that is the space of the created worlds.

Integrated Lights – Truths and understandings that have been apprehended by the mind or heart. As opposed to *Surrounding Lights*.

Israel – Either the area designated by the Bible as the homeland of the Jewish people, or the Jewish people themselves, descendants of Jacob who was also called Israel.

Kabbala – Literally, the received tradition *or* the science of correspondences. That part of the Jewish Oral Tradition which presents the inner and mystical interpretations of the Torah and its practices. It corresponds to the S of PaRDeS.

Katnut – Literally, immaturity. This term is used in kabbalistic writings to indicate a small, narrow, immature mind or state of spiritual development. See *gadlut*.

Kavanna – Intention. The meditative aspect of religious practice—the mindfulness and intention one brings to prayer and mitzvah observance.

Kenesset Yisrael – See Mystical Community of Israel.

Keter –The highest *sefira* and deepest root of the soul, translated as crown. The place where the soul is hewn from the pure simple oneness of God. *Keter* unites God's will with man's will.

Kosher – Something that meets all the stipulations of Jewish law. In particular it is used in relation to dietary requirements.

Lights – Lights are always equivalent to consciousness in kabbalistic writings. Each *sefira* or spark is a light that transmits a particular insight or capacity for awareness.

Malchut – The lowest of the ten *sefirot* is called *malchut* which means literally royalty and kingship. It corresponds to the physical plane and represents the final stage in light's congealing into matter.

Mashiach – Though the Messianic Era will be the fruit of everyone's enlightened efforts, there will still need to be an individual (or couple) to coordinate this massive project of global harmonization. That is the role of *Mashiach* whose spiritual potency and leadership will bring about the final perfecting of Israel and the world..

Mazal Tov – [May it be] a good sign. An expression of congratulations.

Megilla – Literally, "scroll." The book of Esther is one of five biblical books called scrolls because they are each scribed on a roll of parchment and read from that scroll at a public reading on the holiday associated with that book: Esther on Purim; Song of

Songs on Pesach; Ruth on Shavuot; Lamentations on Tisha B'Av; Kohellet on Sukkot.

Mesirut Nefesh – The willingness to suffer ego-death and even physical death for the sake of truth, integrity and the fulfillment of God's will.

Messiah – (see Mashiach)

Messianic Era – A transitional time between *this* world and the next. It begins somewhere towards the end of the sixth millennium (we are now within the period of its likely beginnings) and will take us to the threshold of the world-to-come. It is the joyous stage of actualized perfection. Love of God, love of neighbor and love of Torah reign.

Midda, Middot – Character trait(s), disposition(s). The seven lower *sefirot* or emotive attributes of God (loving-kindness, severity, mercy, etc.).

Midrash, Midrashim – Third level of Biblical interpretation in the model of PaRDeS. Homiletical writings which explain the Biblical text through the use of stories and sermons. The *Midrash* often fills out a sparsely-written Biblical narrative providing background, context, moral lessons or legal implications.

Mitzva, Mitzvot – The 613 commandments of the Written Torah: 365 of which are prohibitions, and 248 of which are required actions. The term *mitzva* is also used colloquially to refer to a good deed.

Mystical Community of Israel – The sum-total of souls comprising the Jewish people (from the beginning of time to its end) that form the inner soul core of creation (from the perspective of the Jewish I-center whose mission is to shine the light of Divine oneness to the world).

Names of God – The No-Thing that is all things, defies name and adjective. Nevertheless Divinity also expresses itself through an infinite variety of attributes. Judaism ascribes different names to these various modes of Divine expression. For example *Havaya* (pronounced *A-donoi*) refers to God's transcendence and *E-lohim* refers to the aspect of God that manifests as nature and natural law.

Nesira- The kabbalistic term for the surgical uncoupling of Eve from Adam. Tradition teaches that Adam and Eve were originally created as a single, bi-gendered creature with male and female halves fused together like Siamese twins. God then severed this bond, releasing them to meet face-to-face as freestanding individuals for the first time. This is how Jewish tradition interprets the biblical story of Eve's formation.

NoThing - The most transcendent and unknowable level of God. The level at which no positive attribute can be ascribed to God, for words and concepts would only project limits onto that which is essentially unlimitable. Also refers to that which precedes the appearance of "thingness" in the creative sequence. The Rootless Root of creation.

Oral Law or Oral Tradition – The explanations and elaborations of the Written Law or Torah. These were also received by Moses at Sinai but passed from mouth to ear, teacher to student, until just after the destruction of the Second Temple. The first recording of the Oral Law was the *Mishna* (180 CE) and this opened the way for all subsequent transcriptions of what ideally was to be a personal, verbal transmission of knowledge and information. Included in the category of the Oral Tradition are the *Mishna, Midrash, Gemara, Talmud* and *Kabbalah.* These are still aspects of the Oral Tradition, even though they are written down. All Jewish teachings besides the Bible itself are considered part of the Oral Tradition.

PaRDeS – Literally, "orchard." Acronym for the four levels of Torah study: *pshat* (plain, literal meaning of the text); *remez* (hints and allusions in the text); *drash* (homiletical levels of meaning derived by verbal analogy), and *sod* (the esoteric, mystical dimension of the text).

Pintila Yid – The fifth and highest level of the Jewish soul, called Yechida, which is hewn from the pure simple oneness of Divinity and confers upon the individual a superrational bond with the Holy *One.*

Principle of Interinclusion – A distinguishing feature of our present spiritual universe is its holographic structure. Every piece contains something of every other piece inside itself. This is always true. No matter how small the fragment, no matter how many subdivisions one executes, the resulting particles always contain a complete set of the whole.

Purim – Rabbinically instituted festival celebrating the miracle by which the Jewish people were saved from genocide during the Persian exile. Based on the Book of Esther.

R. – Short for rabbi, rav, rebbe, rebbetzin (f), rabbanit (f), all of which are variations on a word which means teacher.

Rashi – Acronym for Rabbi Shlomo Yitzchoki, an eleventh century rabbi. The most important commentator on Bible and *Gemara*.

Root Souls – Every soul has a root above that is the place from which it is hewn. Each root soul generally produces a variety of specific expressions on the next level down. Soulmates are souls that derive from a common root soul above.

Rosh Hashanah – Jewish New Year. Occurs on the first day of the seventh month of the Jewish calendar (Tishrei) which generally falls in September or October. It is a day of prayer, reflection and repentance. It is further distinguished as the day for hearing the *shofar*.

Sanhedrin – A Greek word signifying the higher court of law which made rulings on how to interpret and apply the Torah's principles to the practical and evolving circumstances of Jewish life and culture. The Sanhedrin, in spirit, originated with the seventy elders that Moses selected after Sinai. However the formal term, Sanhedrin, refers specifically to the judicial bodies during the Second Temple period. They consisted of seventy members and a president, making seventy-one. The Sanhedrin had jurisdiction over all religious matters.

Sefira / Sefirot – The ten channels of Divine flow and emanation which link the Transcendent Light with Its evolving and apparently finite creation. The ten *sefirot*, as the ten stages in the creative process, are imprinted on all aspects of reality. Seven Noachide Laws – Seven laws (really categories of laws) to which the Torah holds all humanity accountable. They are prohibitions against idolatry, adultery, murder, theft, blasphemy and cruelty to animals and then the proscription to set up courts of justice to regulate the previous six.

Seven-Thousand-Year-Cycle of Biblical History – The Talmud (*San.* 97b) teaches that each creation day translates into 1,000 years of earthly history and the count begins from the appearance of Adam (a creature with specific spiritual capabilities that distinguish him from generic man, or Homo sapiens). The six weekdays are six thousand years of refining ourselves and turning the world into a Temple that can hold and reveal the full presence of God. This period culminates in the messianic time and then transitions into an entirely new era called the world to come or seventh millennium and cosmic Sabbath. At the time of this writing, we are currently in 5768th year of this cycle.

Seven Worlds – See: Eighth Kingdom.

Shabbat – Sabbath. The seventh day of the week from Friday sunset to Saturday night. It is a day of rest from labor and business activity and it is specifically "creative work" (*malacha*) that is forbidden on Shabbat (i.e., the realization of an intelligent purpose by practical skill). There are thirty-nine categories of *malacha* each with many details and particulars. For example, an observant Jew does not cook, light fires (including incandescent lights or the internal combustion engine of a car), sew, write, build, work in the fields and many etceteras. In addition Shabbat is a time to focus on the more spiritual dimension of life. The year 6000 in the Jewish calendar begins the 7th millennium or Sabbath of Creation (we are now in the year 5765).

Shattered Vessels – The chapter of cosmic history that preceded our world was the era of shattered vessels (which is also called the Circle World, the World of Points and the Era of Chaos). Our world is built from the debris of that shattered epoch. The vital souls and bodies of all creation are resurrected sparks and vessels from those shattered worlds.

Shekhina – The feminine expression of Divinity. It means literally Presence, and emphasizes the immanence of God, the indwelling Light that fills all things. The *Shekhina* is that aspect of Hashem that fits inside the universe for all of reality is nothing but Divinity in a state of concealment and contraction.

Shema – Literally, "Hear [Know]." The central declaration of Jewish faith which reads, in English, "Hear (Know) Israel, *God* is our Lord, God is One."

Shulchan Aruch – Code of Jewish Law.

Sin – To act in way that is contrary to spiritual law and God's will as explicated by the Torah. To miss the mark.

Soul – (see also *nefesh*, *ruach*, *neshama*). The spiritual essence of a person or thing; its life force and consciousness. To a certain degree a creature's soul is apparent by its capacity to respond and interact with its environment, and so to manifest a particular range of the infinite continuum of potentialities within Divine consciousness.

Sparks – When the vessels shattered in the World of Chaos, sparks of light embedded in shards tumbled "downward" into the abyss. In each moment some new layer of these fallen sparks rises to vitalize each new moment and all the creatures within it.

String Theory (also Superstrings) – A unified theory of the universe postulating that the fundamental ingredients of nature are not particles but tiny one-dimensional filaments called strings.

Super-rational – Beyond the rational. Reality from God's perspective, which is beyond time and space. This level of awareness actually exists in the unconscious reaches of every person's soul and urges him toward growth and good.

Surrounding Lights – Truths and understandings that are too deep or great for the mind (or vessel) to grasp. As opposed to *Internalized Lights*.

Talmud – The primary repository of the Oral Law, scribed in 499 CE. The Talmud analyzes, develops and interprets the Written Torah in accordance with the explanations that were received, simultaneously with the actual Written Law, by Moses at Sinai.

Tardema- The term used in the Bible to describe Adam's lapse into a deep sleep at Eve's creation (Gen. 2:21); and to describe Abraham's lapse into prophetic reverie at the covenant of the pieces (Gen. 15:12). The term carries both a negative and positive connotation, thus conveying the thin line between unconscious and superconscious awareness.

Ten Commandments – The revelation of Divine will received by the Jewish people at Sinai (recorded on tablets) that form the backbone of Jewish religious values and practices. R. Saadia Gaon shows how these Ten Commandments actually include the entire system of Jewish practice with its 613 obligations.

Teshuva – Literally, *return.* Return to the service of God. The inner, all-consuming commitment to devote one's life to serving God. The process of lower *teshuva* involves acknowledging sins, regretting them and committing to change.

This World – Our physical world where all the laws of nature apply. The state of reality after eating from the Tree Of Knowledge Of Good And Evil and before the world-to-come.

Tikun – A word the means rectification, healing, repair, perfection, elevation . . . all of these at once.

Torah - The first five books of the Bible revealed at Sinai. The word "Torah" often is used to refer to both the written and oral teachings and then denotes the entire body of knowledge generated since Sinai by the Jewish people throughout history.

Tree of Knowledge of Good and Evil – The forbidden tree in Eden that represents a fallen state of consciousness where truth is twisted by emotional attachments and narcissistic needs.

Tsadik / Tsadikim – Literally, righteous, perfect: 1) A person who has purged his or her entire being of all impurity and of every inclination (even subconscious) to act contrary to spiritual law. 2) A person who always behaves properly though wayward impulses do arise. 3) The more righteous person in a dispute. 4) One who believes himself to be the more righteous one even if, objectively, that is not so.

Worlds – refers both to the four planes of reality: physical, emotional, mental, spiritual as well as to the sequential stages in creation's unfolding: Bound World, Circle World and Linear World.

World-To-Come – The seventh millennium and period following the messianic era that marks an entirely new state of existence where physicality, as we know it, dissolves and souls are born into new light bodies wherein they experience an infinitely deepening ecstasy of relationship with God.

Yichuddim – Mystical prayers and meditations that have the power to access the super-conscious lights of pure grace (*Atika*) and draw them down into the lower worlds.

Yom Kippur – Day of Atonement. Climax of the ten-day period of repentance and rededicating one's life to God that begins with *Rosh HaShanah*, the Jewish New Year. Observed as a fast day of prayer and deep devotion where Jews seek and are assured of pardon and forgiveness.

Zohar – Mystical commentary on the Torah. Tradition ascribes its authorship to Rabbi Shimon Bar Yochai and his son, Elazar, around the second century C.E. The Zohar first became known in the thirteenth century. This inspired body of teachings is actually comprised of several works that provide the major source material for the kabbalistic system of thought.

A STILL SMALL VOICE
PRESENTS THE FOLLOWING RESOURCES:

CORRESPONDENCE SCHOOL: A STILL SMALL VOICE is a correspondence school that presents classic Judaism as a powerful path of spiritual transformation. Its weekly lessons draw from all aspects of the Jewish religious tradition; from its most hidden and kabbalistic mysteries to its most basic principles of faith and practice. A year and a half of weekly lessons are currently available: The course titles are: Prayer and Destiny (20 weeks.); The Enlightened Body (12 weeks); Synchrony (13 weeks.); Time Trekking (26 weeks.).

HOMEOPATHIC REMEDY: THE GOLDEN THREAD is a homeopathically produced remedy based on Kabbalah. It is designed to heal the deepest level of soul that was damaged by our collective participation with the Tree of Knowledge of Good and Evil.

KABBALISTIC WRITINGS ON THE NATURE OF MASCULINE AND FEMININE: This book presents a vision of how man and woman will relate when they have healed themselves and fixed the world. Based on a Talmudic tale about the sun and moon; Jewish mystical writings identify seven stages of waning and waxing that mark the feminine life cycle. In the final stage, *woman* stands equal and opposite to *man* and they meet for the first time as spiritual, intellectual and emotional mates. This perfect marriage has been our yearning for six thousand years, and from its consummation flow all promised blessings of the world to come.

EATING AS TIKUN: This book notes that humanities first error was an act of unholy eating (from the Tree of Knowledge), which means that only its opposite can fix it. All of life and all of history are training us for one end: to learn to "eat" in holiness, to not let the world's pleasures wrench our attention from God (even for an instant).

YOU ARE WHAT YOU HATE: **Enemies hold fallen slivers of** our souls, estranged sparks that we do not recognize as pieces of our very own selves. They have chosen us as their opponents because they are trying, in their deluded way, to connect back to their root, which really *is* us. We must collect all the scattered pieces of ourselves, including those currently embedded within our enemy. How do we both protect ourselves and reclaim our sparks? What is the most spiritually productive way to succeed at this paradoxical mission?

EVOLUTIONARY CREATIONISM—**Kabbala Solves the** Riddle of Missing Links: The kabbalistic description of Eden's "fall" presents a scenario of crash and repair that is nearly identical to the account of prehistory derived from the cutting edge of modern physics, called Superstrings. A compelling and intellectually satisfying scenario emerges to explain the evolutionary history of the planet that is perfectly consistent with both Bible and science.

PURIMBURSTS: **This book uses the holiday of Purim to segue into the** deepest kabbalistic mysteries. For example, an excerpt: "This day is called *Purim* because its inner service *is* lots. …One goes deeply inward (and upward) to find a place inside that transcends craving and aversion. Ones love-bond to God gets so deep, one's vision so vast, that the truest (and normally hidden) truth becomes real: Every moment is an opportunity for closeness with God and it is not clear which builds intimacy more, the joy or the pain, the blessing or the curse, Mordechai (the hero) or Haman (the villain). Would there be Purim without Haman? Who do we thank more for this day?"

COUNTDOWN TO PERFECTION—**Meditations on the** Sefirot: Renowned artist, Judith Margolis, illustrates Sarah Yehudit's meditations on the Omer. Available at: www.JudithMargolis.com.

MEDITATION AND LEARNING RETREATS IN JERUSALEM: The goal of these retreats is to create an atmosphere that enables people to access the full healing, guiding, and enlightening potential inherent on Shabbat. There is a wealth of "light" and bounty that comes into the world with Shabbat but for most people this remains an untapped resource. One sure way to harness its potential for healing and transformation is through the practice of retreat.

PRIVATE COUNSELING: In addition to her writing and classroom teaching, Sarah Yehudit spends a significant amount of her time in private teaching and counseling.

RECORDED LECTURE SERIES: Sarah Yehudit Schneider has lectured widely both in Israel and the States. MP3s on a wide variety of topics are available on the Still Small Voice website. For example: Prayer and Destiny; Free Will and Determinism; Judaism and Reincarnation; Messiah and the End of Days; The Secret of the Animals in the Garden of Eden; The Gift of the Oral Torah; What Is A Jew; as well as classes on most of the Jewish festivals. It is also possible to order the recordings of Sarah Yehudit's ongoing classes on Zohar (page by page), Advanced Seminar on Prayer, You are What You Hate, and Mashicah and the End of Days.

TELECONFERENCE CLASSES: In addition to her Jerusalem classes, Sarah Yehudit Schneider teaches weekly telephone classes to the States. To join a preexisting class or to start one of your own, contact: smlvoice@netvision.net.il

---

A STILL SMALL VOICE

Chabad 90/16, Jerusalem, 97500 Israel • tel/fax: (02) 628-2988

smlvoice@netvision.net.il • www.astillsmallvoice.org

A STILL SMALL VOICE is a correspondence school that presents classic Judaism as a powerful path of spiritual transformation. Its weekly lessons draw from all aspects of the Jewish religious tradition; from its most hidden and kabbalistic mysteries to its most basic principles of faith and practice. A year and a half of weekly lessons are currently available:

Prayer and Destiny explores the mystery of prayer and how it is a potent tool for personal and spiritual growth (even more effective than visualization and affirmation). **20 weeks.**

The Enlightened Body shows how the system of Jewish ritual practices is actually a powerful and penetrating spiritual path. **12 weeks.**

Synchrony is an experiential exploration of the six constant *mitzvot*. Among the 613 religious obligations that comprise the Jewish path, six are meditations that one must hold in mind at all times. **13 weeks.**

Time Trekking explores the deeper meanings behind the daily, weekly, monthly and yearly cycles of observance. **26 weeks.**

ENROLLMENT BENEFITS INCLUDE:

- **weekly** lessons of stimulating and practical insights into Jewish wisdom.
- personal guidance through practical exercises that aid integration of the material.
- timely holiday supplements.
- answers to personal questions about lessons, and other topics of Jewish thought.
- **time tested tools guaranteed to enhance peace of mind and quality life.**

APPLICATION FORM
to A Still Small Voice

Name_____

Date _____ Date of Birth _____

Address_____

_____

Tel._____Fax_____

Email_____

Profession_____

Education_____

Please enclose a $15.00 enrollment fee plus tuition:
Israel: $60/quarter (3 mos.) or $210/year
Abroad: $75/quarter (3 mos.) or $260/year
20% discount/person for groups of 5 or more

Payment is valid in foreign currency according to the US$ equivalent.

Mail application or request for more information to:

**A Still Small Voice
Chabad 90/16
Jerusalem 97500
ISRAEL**

See copyright page for the telephone, fax, email, and website of **A Still Small Voice.**

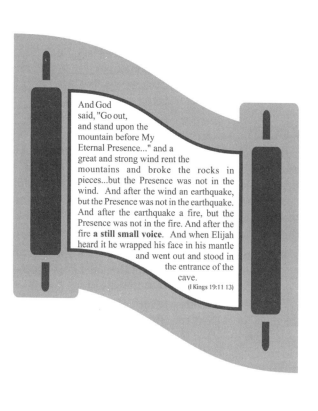

And God
said, "Go out,
and stand upon the
mountain before My
Eternal Presence..." and a
great and strong wind rent the
mountains and broke the rocks in
pieces...but the Presence was not in the
wind. And after the wind an earthquake,
but the Presence was not in the earthquake.
And after the earthquake a fire, but the
Presence was not in the fire. And after the
fire **a still small voice**. And when Elijah
heard it he wrapped his face in his mantle
and went out and stood in
the entrance of the
cave.

(I Kings 19:11 13)

ABOUT THE AUTHOR

Sarah Yehudit (Susan) Schneider is the founding director of A Still Small Voice, a correspondence school that provides weekly teachings in classic Jewish wisdom to subscribers around the world. Sarah is the author of two full-length books entitled: *Kabbalistic Writings on the Nature of Masculine and Feminine* and *You Are What You Hate*. In addition, she has produced several pocket-sized books entitled *Eating as Tikun, Purim Bursts* and *Evolutionary Creationism* as well as numerous essays published in a variety of journals and anthologies.

Sarah Yehudit has a BA in Molecular, Cellular and Developmental Biology from the University of Colorado in Boulder. Since 1981 she has lived in Jerusalem, followed an orthodox path of observance and immersed herself in the study of mystical texts. She also completed the program for advanced study at Neve Yerushalayim Seminary for Women.

Sarah Yehudit teaches a variety of weekly classes throughout Jerusalem, teleconference classes to the States, and offers private instruction to individuals seeking a more personal encounter with text. She also does yearly teaching tours throughout the English-speaking world.